EURYTHMY
FOR THE
YOUNG
CHILD

A GUIDE
FOR TEACHERS
AND PARENTS

ESTELLE BRYER

Editorial Committee: Susan Howard, Stephen Spitalny and Barbara Klocek
Managing Editor: Lydia Roberson
Cover Art: Sheila Harrington
Design and Illustration: Sheila Harrington
Text Editing: Sandy Milczarek and Lydia Roberson
Administrative Support: Janni Nicol and Melissa Lyons

This publication is made possible through a grant
from the Waldorf Curriculum Fund.

© Waldorf Early Childhood Association of North America

First Edition, 2005

Published in the United States by the
Waldorf Early Childhood Association of North America
285 Hungry Hollow Road
Spring Valley, NY 10977

(845) 352-1690

Library of Congress Cataloging-in-Publication Data
0-9722238-5-1
10 9 8 7 6 5 4 3 2 1

Table of Contents

Estelle Bryer

A kindergarten teacher by profession, she became the founding kindergarten teacher at the Constantia Steiner School in Cape Town, South Africa in 1960 and has been there in various capacities ever since. She studied and then taught eurythmy in both Michael Oak and the Constantia Schools in Cape Town (for children aged three to eighteen years old). In 1980, she studied eurythmy therapy in Stuttgart, Germany. She then became a eurythmy therapist, but all the while specialising in kindergarten eurythmy for ages three to seven. Estelle semi-retired from the schools in 2004, but still supervises eurythmy therapy.

Estelle is a master puppeteer and performs in a variety of private and public venues. She also established the well-known permanent Rainbow Puppet Theater. She still lectures extensively on aspects of the young child, parenting, grandparenting, eurythmy and puppetry.

WORDS FOR BOTH KINDERGARTEN AND EURYTHMY TEACHERS

What follows in this book is the fruit of forty-three years of working with the kindergarten child in Steiner Waldorf education. The first fourteen years as kindergarten teacher, then as eurythmy teacher from 1974-1980. From 1982, I also worked as eurythmy therapist specializing in the young child age group. I have five kindergarten classes per week, two of three- to four-year-olds (ten to fifteen children per class) and three of four- to six-and-a-half-year olds (twenty to twenty-three per class). In my spare time, I am an enthusiastic puppeteer doing shows far and wide for the same age group. I sometimes give courses on the above at the Kindergarten Teacher Training Seminar and at the Eurythmy School.

Out of the above experience, it is usually easy for me to work out of the spontaneous needs of the children, but the modern child has different needs and has changed over the years. It is heartbreaking to see the effects of the modern rushed, arrhythmic, technical life and the distressing collapse of the family structure on more and more children.

Etheric forces are depleted and one now more often hears, "I'm tired," and some children cannot maintain their uprightness nor raise their arms without their hands flopping. More kindergarten children than ever are in need of eurythmy therapy.

Circle time in the kindergarten is becoming more therapeutic and more consciously structured.

Many of the lessons in this book have been used as a basis for circle time. They, on the whole, have all the necessary components. Some of the verses may be removed from the stories and used on their own or elsewhere. The verses in the Verse section have all been used at one time or another and work well.

For the kindergarten teacher, it is important to read through all that is written for the eurythmy teacher for there is much there that applies to general kindergarten work as well as to circle time.

Many of the stories are also suitable and have been used for Grade 1 eurythmy lessons, (e.g. *Golden Goose*, *Michaelmas*, *Big Blue Boat*), but here the movements are expected to be more formed.

Although there is a wealth of information about child development and the requirements of every age, this book has another outline with comments on their needs in Morning Circle and Eurythmy Classes. The kindergarten teacher must ignore the eurythmy indications and carry out the lessons "normally." They adapt and work well.

Music for the numbered verses can be found begining on page 113.

NOTES FOR EURYTHMISTS

Where letters give the indications for movements are upper case, it means LARGE movements. And the lower case letters mean small gestures, (e.g. **U u**).

These are indications only. Please feel free to do your own gestures and experiment.

Pronunciation of vowels:

A Ah (father)

E Ay (fame)

I Ee (feet)

O Aw (dawn)

U Oo (moon)

Working with the Development of the Child

The child is born out of the spiritual world with an attitude of complete devotion as if to say, "Everything is new to me. I must learn from everyone and everything, but I am sure that this world is good and true and beautiful. I will take everything into myself. I can sense how people think, how they feel, how they walk and move because I am right inside them. I am inside all of nature and part of it. I am the wind, the flowers, the water. Nothing is outside of me. Through my God-given power of imitation, I absorb all as if I am one big sense organ with no boundaries. The same as when people, in deep prayer, give themselves over to God in utter spiritual devotion, so do I give myself over to the world and all that is in it."

Every eurythmist knows (because it is an integral part of the training) how the entire human being is connected with the zodiac and planets. The structure of the body is connected with the forces of the Zodiac, and the inner organs with the planets—kidneys (Venus), lungs (Mercury), reproductive organs (Moon), gall bladder (Mars), liver (Jupiter), spleen (Saturn) and the heart (Sun).

The incarnating child inherits its physical body and spends the years until the change of teeth in transforming this inherited body, with all its vital organs, into its own: For this, the child uses all that it absorbs through gesture—the gestures of the thinking, feeling and actions of all the human beings in the perceived environment and of nature, also, unfortunately, of the modern technical/mechanical world. Gesture/movement belongs to the etheric (life) body, and it is the etheric body that is predominantly active in this transformation process. Because each vowel and consonant is connected with the Zodiac and planets, the eurythmy movements for these, being so true, have a very deep and healing effect on this transformation process.

In learning to stand, to speak and to think in the first three years, the child is under the direct guiding forces of spiritual beings, the ego of the child remaining outside its body. When the child begins to say "I," the ego incarnates for the first time.

In the first seven years, the incarnation process proceeds in two directions: the growth process from the head through the chest/rhythmic system (approx. four to five years) and through the limbs (approx. five to seven years). During this last phase, the limbs elongate. There is some truth in the old Eastern test for school-readiness that only when the child can put his arm over his head and touch his ear, with his head upright, is the growth phase complete. The etheric body is then released from its specialized task of transformation. It is then free to be used for memory proper. (However, with large-headed children, this does not always apply.)

The other functional developmental process from willing to feeling to thinking, goes in the opposite direction, from the limbs, through the chest to the head. Although during the entire period from birth to change of teeth the child is in the "will," which is all activity, so within this period there are also divisions. Both of these streams meet in the rhythmic system just before the age of four years and that is when the fantasy awakes, and the child is ready for fairy tales. Thinking awakens between the ages of five and seven years. With the change of teeth, the thinking transformation is freed from the head.

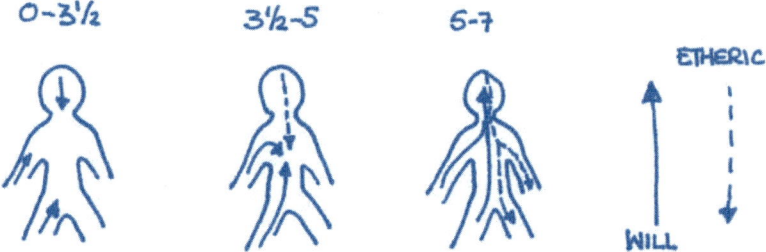

One generally sees these incarnation processes in children's drawings as circles and spirals "in space" which become "head-men" with stick arms protruding from the head, to repetitive lines and forms when the growth forces reach the rhythmic system. At this stage, the house (representing the physical body) begins to float down until it becomes earthed. Then more detail and figures surround and eventually enter the house and, with the development of thinking, the roof becomes triangular.

Until fantasy awakens, eurythmy and circle time should be about everyday things that are familiar to the children such as gardening, baking, washing, farming—and more with the idea in mind, "This is how things work and live on this earth," e.g. "Look, if I let my knees kiss each other like this..., and put my hands behind me to make a tail like this..., then I can waddle just like a duck." (Then follows a duck song or verse). Sentences should be short and there can be much repetition. They need not keep to a circle and all is imitation, e.g. "My feet are so close together that they can kiss each other." Consciousness is still dreamy, and their movements are out of the forces of sympathy. Some children are so inside the teacher's movements that they hardly ever move themselves.

When the child is about four-years-old, one can begin with simple repetitive fairy tales, e.g. *The Turnip*. More and more, one can capture them within the realm of fantasy, e.g. "And of course he put his feet together and stood straight when he spoke to the prince..." Four-year-olds live in a dream-like way with their surroundings, but their little limbs are wide-awake and active, and they are on the go all the time. As the children grow, stories in eurythmy class or in circle time can then become more complicated.

When children are school-ready, the teacher can become more authoritative and expect the children to be more correct and qualitative in their movements. Here nods of recognition can do wonders.

Once the children are in Grade One, the eurythmy teacher can expect more controlled, more conscious movement from the children. Now the teacher becomes an authority, and the more they love the teacher, the better the quality of the lesson will be for they will want to please.

At all ages, the children are at one with nature, the weather and the seasons, and stories may be so adapted to this. Contraction and expansion belong to the healthy human being every bit as much as to nature and the year (spring/summer—expansion, autumn/winter—contraction), etc. and should be brought into the planning of the lessons and be done within the lessons. This can be done as finger-rhymes as well as in loud and soft, opening and closing (with hands, arms and as a circle) sleeping and waking, in and out and all contrasts. The more the teacher can have an awareness of this hidden background, the deeper will it work into the being of the children.

The Eurythmy Lesson
Beginning the Lesson

There are many ways of forming eurythmy lessons for the little ones. Here are some suggestions of ways that work for me. If the children come to the eurythmy room, and there is the possibility of them waiting outside in an ante-room then, when all are quiet and holding hands, the front child can knock three times on the door. The eurythmy teacher immediately opens the door and leads them into a circle, holding the front child by the hand. The advantage of this way is that the children are very quiet and orderly from the beginning and there is an air of magic and expectancy when the door opens. I stand inside at the door, waiting. Another method that I used in the lower classes to get the children quiet and ready is to give the responsibility to the class teacher.

The following verse to lead them in can either be spoken or sung:

1

Here we go, on tip-toe,
Over the rainbow-bridge we go.
Treading softly, treading slow (so)
Over the rainbow-bridge we go.
Up into the heavens far,
Gathering light from sun and star,
Down to earth all things to greet,
Bringing light to all we meet.
One can enter to music, if one is fortunate enough to have a musician.

The three- to four-year-olds cannot be expected to form a circle. To overcome this, one can lead them in holding hands, but facing the outside with their backs towards the circle center, then jump around to face the center. For them to keep a circle is not important.

Another way to lead them in is not to hold hands, but for them to follow the eurythmy teacher with that wonderful old German folk song which Rudolf Steiner suggested for the English Nursery eurythmy class—to be done with soul-gestures. The children love this, and, if not used to lead them in, it can be done to lead the lesson to a close.

2

Adam he had seven sons,
Seven sons had he,
They would not eat,
They would not drink,
But all went just like me.

With arms up, we walk (skip or tiptoe, etc.) around the room singing, but, with the last line, "But all went just like me," we skip with the soul-gesture of merriment, or walk with piety, or stamp with greed, the last time treading softly with inwardness... to end quietly with reverence.

Another verse:

3

This is the way to (eurythmy land) (3x)
This is the way to eurythmy land,
We go by the light of the moon.

When the children are all quiet in the circle the following is my routine. The kindergarten child needs ritual, so I made a "golden" bottle in which I put rose oil with a tiny bit of extra rose-essence, so that it really smells of roses, but the smell is delicate. Then, holding the bottle in my right hand (being right-handed) and the child's right hand (palm up) in my left, I put their palm over the top of the bottle and up-end it so that just a little bit goes onto their palm. In this way I go around the circle singing:

4

Roses, roses give your oil,
Roses, roses from the soil,
Roses, roses give your light,
Roses of delight.

Then we all gently rub our palms together and smell them. Being aware that whatever I feel of reverence is absorbed deeply into the child through their God-given gift of imitation, I gently rub my palms together and take a deep, deep in breath of my hands, I then let the rose-perfume penetrate right through me to my toes. Sometimes I make a remark or question: "I wonder how this wonderful perfume gets into the roses!?" or "Thank you, Father Sun." Sincerity, gratitude and devotion are all-important.

This ritual is also important for child observation, as one can feel which children have warm or cold hands, strength of the hands, which child can look you in the eye, etc. Much can reveal itself. Also, it is a good time for children to learn good manners for they can each say, "Thank you," quietly when receiving the oil.

After this, we all stand with feet together and listen to the golden gate opening (interval of the fifth played three times on chime-bars or lyre or any other pure pentatonic instrument). In this way there is an education of the senses of smell and hearing. Sometimes we also do the interval of the fifth with our arms.

The lesson proper then begins with an opening verse, followed by the main story.

ENDING THE LESSON

There are verses to bring the lesson to a close and the children to quietness. When all are quiet with their feet together, the interval of the fifth can be played again—to close the Golden Gate. This forms a wholeness with the beginning.

It is important for the children to rest quietly at the end of the lesson. This can be done all standing quietly with feet together or, because of today's hectic lifestyle that makes children tire so quickly, I have introduced the following with great success:

After the Golden Gate is played, we all take a step back and lie down on our tummies. (This is easy if one has a carpet.) Then we make a pillow with our arms and lay our cheek on it. I play very soft music with single tones, and all listen to make their ears magic so that they will be able to hear the flowers grow, or the leaves fall, etc. After a while, they change ears to make the other ear magic. I tail off the music so that they lie absolutely still in total silence. I am sure that this has a healing effect on the sense of hearing, which has to put up with so much cacophony and artificiality in our modern life. Also, it is wonderful when all the children lie very quietly with not even one foot moving; it creates a mood of peace that we are all reluctant to break.

Again, this is a time for observation as to how restless some children are.

Slowly we then get up while I sing:

4

Slowly, slowly, up we stand,
Take each other by the hand, (repeat)

We then go out singing:

This is the way from eurythmy land, etc.

or:

5

Puffer train, puffer train, quiet little puffer train.
When you come from eurythmy,
Puffer train then quiet be, (sshh—sshh—sshh) (2x)
Quiet little puffer train.
If there is a birthday, the birthday child leads in and out.

In Lecture Four of the *Supplementary Course*, Rudolf Steiner has the following to say about the closing of a eurythmy lesson. This applies to all ages.

When the child does eurythmy, he comes into movement; and the spiritual that is in the limbs streams upwards on the path of the child's movements. We set the spiritual free when we give the child eurythmy. (And it is the same with singing.) The spiritual, with which the limbs are full to overflowing, is released. This is a real process that takes place in the child. We draw away the spiritual—we call it forth. And then when the child stops doing the exercises, the spiritual that we have called forth is, so to speak, waiting to be used. The spiritual is also waiting to be established, to be secured. We must meet this need.

We have, you see, "spiritualized" the child. Through doing gymnastics, eurythmy, or singing, he has become a different being. He has in him much more of the spiritual than he had before. This spiritual element in him wants to be established, wants to remain with him; and it is for us to see that it is not diverted. There is a very simple way of doing this. After the lesson is finished, let the children remain quiet for a little. Give the whole class a rest, and make sure that during this time—it need only be a very few minutes—they are quiet and undisturbed. The older the children, the greater the need for this pause. We must never forget to provide for it; if we do forget then, on the following day, we shall fail to find in the children what we need.

CLOTHING AND VOICE

Ideally, the children should all have tunics with the color indicated by Rudolf Steiner as shades of fresh green, and eurythmy shoes, but this is not always possible. Fresh green has the complimentary color of peach-blossom which is the color of love; this is the natural color for this age group. The complimentary color before the change of teeth has the stronger working on the being of the child.

To have the bare feet enclosed, especially with eurythmy shoes, makes a difference. The lesson is much more special if they have to prepare for it, and dressing up belongs to this age.

The indication also is that the eurythmy teacher wears white. (When I wear pale colors or white with pale flowers painted on the material, the children always remark that I "look pretty.")

The voice of the teacher should at all times be natural. One can deepen for a bear or take on certain tinges, but not be "artificial." Being unnatural will irritate the children.

Because children imitate, if one uses a quiet voice, the children will also be quiet.

The more one can fill the spoken word with the qualities of the sounds they contain the better, e.g. there is a reason why the word light has an "h" in it even though it is usually not consciously sounded—it gives the word a "spirit content."

DISTURBANCES DURING THE LESSON

Not all lessons go as smoothly as one would like. When this happens, the first thing I do is question myself. Have I prepared sufficiently? Do I know the verses well enough so that I can be with the children? Has the theme gone on too long? Is it the full moon? Is the wind blowing too strongly? Next, I question the teacher about how the children have been prior to the lesson and why particular children are acting up. If at all possible, one should find out from the kindergarten teacher beforehand whether there is any child who needs particular care, and why.

Children who are uncomfortable in their bodies, due to low muscle-tone or lack of structure, sometimes say "I'm tired" in the middle of the lesson. They can sit on a chair and watch and, depending on the child, be told to watch how nicely the hands or arms speak. They can also be included from time to time by asking them, "Did you see that?"

There are those children who pull and push and bump others, or exaggerate movements and "try to be funny." These would do well to be placed between two older girls or next to a teacher. No doubt, there are not the proper home-boundaries to nourish the sense of touch, or they watch too much television or computer games. Eurythmy therapy may be the answer here. If there is a child who continuously disturbs, no matter what, and has to be put out of the circle, it is important to bring them in positively at the end.

The three-year-olds will not be caught up in fantasy and will sometimes interrupt with "news" that has nothing to do with the lesson. One can listen to the comment then, before the other children add theirs, to quickly divert their attention, e.g. the "Kirri-kirri" verse below.

The six-year-olds, who are school-ready and have gained mastery over their limbs, will accept authority, a "strong look," a whisper in the ear, or positive comments about how well they can do something. More can be expected from them and soft comments such as, "Good, you're putting your feet down neatly," to one child can bring immediate responses from all.

What is all-important is *never to let go of one's consciousness of the group while dealing with the individual child*. Also, as much as possible one must be centered and confident for children will pick up uncertainty immediately.

Guided movement, such as in the eurythmy lesson or circle time, reveal how well or otherwise the children are incarnated, for this touches the very core of that process. Through rhythm, balance, and coordinated movement, more can be revealed about the child than at any other time. This applies to eurythmy lessons throughout the school, where, in most cases, one finds that the children who do not like eurythmy are the ones who are not well incarnated.

A eurythmy therapist can often gauge where the problem lies and can be called upon to help.

What works very well to call children's attention is my "magic finger." No matter how noisy a class is, this has worked. I lift my little finger up fairly high, ignore the children, look at my finger and sing:

6
Kirrikirriki, sing ki-ki, little finger you tell me,
Kirrikirrikoo, sing koo-koo, little finger tell me true.

Then I listen to my finger that knows *everything* and say, e.g. "My little finger says you are making too much noise." or "My little finger says that he'd like to see Tommy standing properly." Of course, this must not be done too often, or it will lose its novelty. One can go over to a flower and say: "Ssshh, the flower wants to tell me something. (listen) She says you are making a noise and it makes her head sore!"

STRUCTURE OF THE LESSON

Regular rhythm is a necessity in the pre-school child. Lessons should be not more than once a week. "The children should be full of joyful expectation and look forward to their lesson; it would be detrimental if this was not the case, if they were overfed with eurythmy." (R. Steiner). I give regular classes on a Monday, but find the children (and myself) much more responsive and creative on a Wednesday, Thursday, or Friday.

The lessons are built up rhythmically: a quiet beginning, then the main body of the lesson which has its own contraction and expansion within it, and a quiet ending with a rest at the end. The stories can continue for weeks and can have variations within them, e.g. the dwarfs can put different animals to bed in winter. Or, one can stick to the same words each week. With longer stories, e.g. *The Golden Goose*, one can build up the story over weeks until the end, each time repeating parts of it.

As soon as the children know the wording of the verses well, they want to speak them. One notices then that the arms go down and one sees how the "creative word dies into speech." We then take out our "golden keys" and lock our mouths and only speak with our arms "as the angels do." Only the teacher then speaks.

On the last lesson of the story, when the children know it really well, we sometimes speak only with our arms with no words at all to accompany. Sometimes there can be a word or two softly here and there if necessary, but the children usually respond well to this, and the quiet movements come *really* alive.

MUSIC

A selection of instruments is ideal. I have pentatonic chime-bars, a small (metal) and a large (wooden) glockenspiel, and a pentatonic lyre. These can be used as an adjunct to a piano (if one has one). I have removed the **C** and **F** keys of the glockenspiels to make them pentatonic.

The kindergarten teacher sits on the side and plays them. She has to be schooled in their use in order to get the mood of the fifth.

The fifth interval of the "Golden Gate" has to be properly carried (I like the chime bars for this). One of my teachers, who is good at sensing the needs of the class when she feels it warranted, plays the "falling fifth." It is interesting to experience and also to move the difference. The fifth has a healthy forming influence on the young child and one should show it to the children with devotion.

The world forms man.
Man within the Divine.
In experiencing the fifth, man perceives himself within the divine world order.
—R. Steiner.

When there is no possibility of music—sing!

VOWELS AND CONSONANTS

In the first seven years, the young child is constantly in the process of transforming the inherited physical body into its own. Hence the formative power of the consonants is what is most needed to imitate.

Nora von Baditz, who was kindergarten eurythmist at the time of Rudolf Steiner, has the following to say:

The first eurythmy with children under the age of seven began with the remark of Dr. Steiner: "If eurythmy is done with small children under the age of seven they will develop the ego-force (Ich-kraft) which neither school nor karma can bring about." Later: "Now ego and astral body are built up from below when the whole man is drawn into the educational process. A powerful ego-feeling would, for instance, come into being if one should introduce the child to elementary eurythmy between the third and fourth years of his life. Then the human being would be claimed by it and this would thrust a right *ego-feeling into his being."*

On the following day after this talk, I began with a group of small children. The only indication for the lessons with children of this age was to do "primitive" eurythmy. There is a remark of Dr. Steiner's that eurythmy in general links up with those forces that are working in the child before the third year. Those who have meditatively thought about the first three years and studied the lectures, The Spiritual Guidance of Man and Humanity, *will be able to understand how these two remarks are linked together and will realize the immense value of eurythmy being done with children as early as possible. Therefore, one should begin about the third year—or even earlier.*

The teacher must have a creative happiness and vitality enabling her/him to adjust to the children in a sanguine way without asking them for results, or, which would be quite impossible, correcting them. They should experience nothing but happiness in the world of eurythmy. How simple everything has to be is expressed by the word "primitive" eurythmy. It has been hard to find out what is meant by it, however, the children showed exactly what was right for them and I learned from each lesson. They rejected everything that had to do with thinking and counting, that is they could not do it. For instance, when I wanted to do "short, short, long," some did four times short, others two or three times long. I could see that one has to keep to one element at a time. They have to be completely free, I thought, in order to be able to enter into the activities each in their own way. Never should the children be compelled to do a thing, everything should come out of joyful and loving imitation of all movements...When I asked Dr. Steiner whether it is good to do fairy tales in eurythmy at this age, he said: "This will be very good; fairy tales should only be done in rhythms, never in prose."

As everything at this age is directed towards the healthy development of the physical body towards removing its obstacles, the lessons should be organized in such a way that the eurythmy can penetrate the feet, preventing flat feet, penetrate the fingers, regulate the forces of life and growth of the teeth thus preventing decay, widen the chest, regulate the breath and stimulate digestion. In short, they keep the child healthy. While working with the children, the teacher is aware of all these influences; he/she will see to it that light, life and love penetrate his/her soul so that the children will experience only health-bringing forces. Our own soul attitude in the surrounding of the children may be of a healing or destructive nature influencing these organs, tissue and blood circulation.

I find the above quotations most helpful.

Primitive eurythmy for me can also be that one feels more and more the primal source of the sounds and their connection with the Zodiac and the planets, and also the connection with the eurythmy figures as given by Rudolf Steiner, so that it eventually becomes as second nature to be a representative of the *Cosmic Word*. There is a nice phrase that I once heard: "To be the mid-wife between the Creative Word and the child."

The most important consonant is **B**. One can well understand that this sound, from the constellation Virgo, surrounds and protects children like a blue mantle of heaven. This movement is also of great value therapeutically when a child has incarnation difficulties, particularly in this era when the home-life is so disrupted.

The only time I ever use **I (ee)** is at Christmas time when we jump for joy. "It's Christmas!," and then never with the *fully* extended movement. **I** does not belong to this age, as the prime mood is *gratitude and thankfulness* which will lead the child to the love of God. The emphasis of the ego by means of the **I** therefore has no place. I use **I** with fingers and sometimes with the feet.

The children *love* doing **F.** So much so that I often extend words to exaggerate and repeat the sound, e.g. f-f-f-fishes, f-f-f-fire, f-f-f-flames, f-f-f-flag.

The **T** is also magical and they love doing it so that one can easily capture them with it, e.g. if they are running or skipping then..."STop!"

L and **M**. It is always so affirming to see how these two wonderfully healing movements have their immediate effect at this age. **L** and **M** (as one knows from eurythmy therapy), have to do with breathing. This causes some of the children to start yawning! With the **M** in particular, I let them go on and on without a sound, e.g. mixing bread or cake or swimming. The unspoken sound then permeates the whole room with its healing quality. It is also amazing how well they manage through imitation.

The children also yawn with **A (ah)**, that is *the* most open gesture.

With the sound **R**, I also exaggerate at times when wheels go rrrrround and rrr-round and rrrrroll it on my tongue. The children cannot help copying the sound, and I encourage this as it activates the speech organs. It is the only sound they say while at the same time doing the movement.

The **reverence E (ay)** with arms folded should be done sparingly and with the mood of reverence, and then it will have a profound effect. To cross the arms over the breast often, (as one sometimes sees when children walk in line in the lower classes), can blunt against the effect of humility.

Duration of the Lesson

For the younger group, ten to fifteen minutes is sufficient depending on the age (three to four years). One may have to do a section in the middle of the lesson with the class sitting, as these little ones get tired easily. If they lie down after the closing, this can add a further five minutes or so. For the older group, the lesson should be about twenty minutes, but I mostly stretch it further depending on the enthusiasm and what we are doing, e.g. the "horse-training," (see page 102) which they love. This they sometimes even continue on in their play. The rest time, if they lie down, is a further five minutes. One has to gauge from their reactions, as some children have healthier life forces than others.

The main thing is that the children should not get overtired, and the lessons must be joyous so that they look forward to them. Happy the teacher where the children ask the mother in the morning, "Is it eurythmy today?" or "How many sleeps till eurythmy?" and want to come to school even if ill.

What has puzzled me for years was that some children referred to the lesson as "Me-rythmy" until it dawned on me that "You-rythmy" to the child could become "Me-rythmy" from their point of view!

The Role of the Kindergarten Teacher in the Eurythmy Lesson

With the three- to four-year-olds, it is always nice when the kindergarten teacher can join in because at this age she is like the mother hen encompassing her chickens, providing the etheric sheath for them. If she does join in, she must do her utmost to fill her movements with quality when imitating the eurythmy teacher and to "be one of the children" but at the same time to quietly be there next to any child who needs extra structuring. If there are musical instruments to be played, she can sit quietly behind them at the side/back of the room. It would be good if she could practice music for the basics: bear walk, mouse, dwarfs, skipping rhythms, bunny jumps, etc.

It is interesting to note how the classes differ according to the qualities of the kindergarten teachers when there is more than one class to a school. In some countries, as here in South Africa, there is one teacher for eighteen to twenty-three children per class. This, believe it or not, has its advantages. Because at this age one can carry them so strongly through imitation, and they are not yet too individualized, I once tried three classes combined (sixty children!) and it worked. There is one class where the teacher is so "together" and she and I are so attuned, that the lesson sometimes functions on a much higher level. After such a lesson she and I both know what has happened and are filled with gratitude. Even her playing of the fifth (Golden Gate) on the chime bars has a different quality and penetrates far deeper than the equivalent from other teachers.

At What Age Can the Child Start Eurythmy?

Nora von Baditz, who taught eurythmy to young children under the guidance of Rudolf Steiner, wrote:

The earlier a child starts to experience the benefits of eurythmy, the more it will benefit him. Dr. Steiner answered the question of a mother as to whether it would be good for her little daughter of one-and-a-half-years to have private lessons in eurythmy: "Yes, that is right. One cannot begin too early with eurythmy." So one could surely begin with group eurythmy before the third year. Dr. Steiner's words should always be kept in mind: "Eurythmy lengthens the span of activity of those forces which hold sway in the child before the third year." Which forces are these? It is the force of Christ that rules in the child up to the third year. In His service, the eurythmy of the small child should be guided, leading it in all humility to "the new Lord of the Earth." We are continuing the work of the Gods.

Steiner says:

Let us think of the child, the incomplete human being, who has not yet attained to his full manhood. How shall we help the gods, so that the physical form of the child shall be rightly furthered in its development? What shall we bring to the child in the way of movement? We must teach him eurythmy, for this is a continuation of divine movement, of the divine creation of man. And when illness of some kind or another overtakes the human being, then the forms corresponding to his divine archetype receive injury; here, in the physical world, they become different. What shall we do then? We must go back to those divine movements; we must help the sick human being to make those movements for himself. This will work upon him in such a way that the harm his bodily form may have received will be remedied.

Gesture and Movement During Circle Time

Why not eurythmy gestures?

Kindergarten teachers have at times voiced the question: "What kind of gestures must we do with our poems and songs? Can we do eurythmy gestures?" Over the years I have witnessed teachers trying to illustrate poems with eurythmy gestures which have been more like semaphor waving—well thought out, but empty. We know that the child in the first seven years is an imitative being who learns through imitating movement and gesture, but it is the quality within the gesture that is all-important. Gesture should never be empty, but filled with quality, intention and feeling.

Many years ago at a Kindergarten Teachers' Conference, Dr von Kugelgen, the "father" of the Steiner Waldorf Kindergarten Movement, explained that to do un-descriptive, unfilled eurythmy gestures made no sense. He used the example that doing all the vowel gestures for "Golden sun in heaven blue" would not be nearly as effective as opening the arms to the imaginary sun while imagining the warmth and glory of it and all that it means for the earth, and filling the movement with this gratitude.

Rudolf Steiner said that it takes seven years to become a eurythmist. In the four-year training course, one learns thoroughly through movement how the vowels, which express our inner life, are related to the planets; e.g. the sound **Ah** is connected to Venus, the quality of Venus is love and loving sacrifice. When we say **Ah** our throat is at its most open. As a gesture, we do this naturally without thinking when we open our arms to welcome someone coming towards us. In eurythmy, we make this gesture consciously for that sound by imbuing it with open loving feeling and bringing it so to life that it carries the physical without gravity in a conscious flowing movement while, at the same time, having as a background the planetary qualities, planetary movement and also the three colors and tension points which Rudolf Steiner gave for each sound. Every sound has a foundation such as this and nothing is arbitrary.

The consonants are connected to the zodiac signs in the same way. They are also related to the four elements e.g. **f, s, sh**: fire, **r**: air, **b, p, d**: earth, etc. What the speech organs do are translated into the equivalent descriptive movement and these movements can be done qualitatively with almost any part of the body, e.g. fingers, legs, shoulders, feet, elbows.

The kindergarten eurythmy teacher uses few movements, but each one is thoroughly penetrated with the above. These are "primal" movements. These qualities are cultivated through endless practice, which permeate the gestures with the healing and up-building substance that the child takes as living imitation. (This is why it is so important for children to have eurythmy before the change of teeth. They imitate cosmic movement!)

Eurythmy therapy is a further study in how to adapt the movements and allow them to penetrate even deeper as a healing for many ailments. But this should be done in conjunction with a doctor wherever possible.

What Movements Should the Teacher Do?

The teacher should find descriptive gestures that fit the meaning of the song/ verse and make them as beautiful as possible, not resort to eurythmy gestures. The teacher should at all times be conscious of the beauty, the purity and truth of the gesture. It should be filled with the soul of the teacher, and weave etheric forms. The child will imitate not only the physical gesture, but also the etheric form that is created. The outreached arms embrace, the butterfly of the waving hands cause currents in the air around the fingers, and the upward stretch reaches to the heavens, connecting with what is beyond the fingers.

The teachers must also do clapping, stamping, vigorous, quiet, tip-toe, walking on heels, skipping, hopping finger-games and more. Contrasts are important between loud and soft, contraction and expansion, tension and relaxation. The possibilities are endless.

The "filled" gesture is important at other times as well. For instance, when lighting a candle…to make a beautiful "rainbow bridge" gesture with the flame to the wick, or, when setting the table, to put the dishes down with care and precision. In passing the food graciously, in opening ones arms when calling a child, or beckoning, or even the way one lifts a chair, greets a friend or a parent.

The gesture of speech is also important, for it is the clarity of our consonants that help to structure the children. It is how you say the words that is as important as the meaning within them.

When doing animal movements such as a bear walking or, as in the Peter stories (see *Summer* and *Fill-in Stories*), the various animals chewing, the teacher must try to creep into the movement of the animal from within, so that one feels as if one is actually the tortoise chewing. Movement belongs to the etheric kingdom, and it is the etheric that the child imitates.

We need to hold a consciousness in our thought, word, gesture and deed which will form not only a healthy image for the child to imitate, but help form the healthy physical of the child.

The task of the teacher is certainly not an easy one, but it is the striving to better ourselves that also penetrates the children and gives them a firm foundation for the rest of their lives.

ACTUAL LESSONS

All are suitable for Kindergarten age
- ✎ suitable for three-and-a-half-year-olds (may be shortened)
- ❁ suitable for Grade 1.

SPRING

The spring rains came,
(kneel and drum fingertips on the floor)

Listen to the rain, on the windowpane
Pitter-patter, pitter-patter,
There it goes again.
(drum palms on the floor)

Rain (4x) on the rooftops
Rain (4x) on the rooftops
P-o-u-r-ing (or th-u-n-der) (faster drumming—even use fists)

All sit and repeat the above verses using first toes, then flat feet. Then repeat again using hands and feet together. This can be used in many lessons with different themes.

Go, little gnome, and see if you can hear
The snowdrops ringing loud and clear.
A little gnome crept from his home (from crouching to standing with **O** above head)
Methinks I hear a raindrop near (**I [ee]** with pointer finger right hand)
Drip, drop, drip, drop, drizzle on the treetop, (**D** 5x, **T** on head then shoulders)
Rain (4x), I go back in my home again. (**R, O** to squatting again)
Go again little gnome, it's stopped raining.

Repeat verse.

But the next time the rain had stopped and what did he hear?
Snowdrops!

7
Ding, dong, ding, dong, ding, dong, ding,
Little bells are ringing,
Ding, dong, ding, dong, ding, dong, ding,
Little bells are singing,
(hands together in front all the time, moving from side to side, sing)

Touch the moon and touch the stars,
Hear the angels a-singing,
Night is coming from a-far
Hear the little bells ringing.

Down went the little gnome,
"The snowdrops are ringing," he said
"Go up and see if the bluebells are ringing."

The little gnome crept from his home, (rise up with **O**)
And what did he hear?
Ding, dong, ding, dong. (hands wide out, then swing together)

Repeat with music or singing, tone lower than "snowdrops."

Down went the gnome, "The blue-bells are ringing," he said.
"Go up and see if the church-bells are ringing."

The little gnome crept from his home. **O**
Ding, dong, ding, dong. (feet apart, hands together, swing through legs and up)

Down went the gnome, "The church-bells are ringing," he said.

Up came ALL the gnomes to listen. (alternate between all the various bells)
"It's springtime! It's springtime!" (jump with **I** or **P**)
Now it was time to wake the animals.

The leaves were rustling and a little nose was twitching. (twitch nose)

"Wake up, wake up, the sun shines bright, **E A EA A**

The dark is conquered by the light." **D KK L** (also with arms and legs together)

The little rabbit opened one eye and looked around,
Then he opened the other eye and looked around,
"Oh," he said, "Is it springtime already? **P**
Thank you little dwarfies for looking after me." And off he hopped.

Rabbit can also talk with his ears—small sounds by head. **E U DFFFF U A**

The above formula can be used with variations for any animal, insect, etc., e.g. beetle.

"Wake up...light." (repeat)
"Is it springtime already?" said the beetle, "Thank. . .me."
"Please, would you mind polishing my back so that I will be all shiny for spring?"
(polish) **SSH**

When it's the bear's turn, the dwarfs are scared. What happens if he is having a bad dream? Who will be brave enough to wake him?

"Me!" (**I** with one finger) *said a little dwarf.* (repeat softly) *"Wake up...light." The bear growled* **Rrrr** *loudly. All went quickly down, and their knees were knocking together, "I will," said another little dwarf.* (repeat louder with same reaction) *"Let us all try together."* (repeat even louder, then quickly down)

The bear opened his eyes and looked around.
"Is it springtime already? Thank you little dwarfies for looking after me." And off he went.
(bear walk)

Then the dwarfs clean the caves.

This is the way we (sweep the caves) (3x) *(Mulberry Bush tune)*
To get them nice and clean.
Polish the floors, wash the windows, scrub, etc. **SH W R,** *etc.*
Then they play a game.
We hide behind a bush (down **B** over head) *Where are you? Here we are!* (repeat)

Gardening ✤

Most of this is done to the tune of *Mulberry Bush*. The following can be done in parts, selected, moved around or improvised on.

A boy and girl (came skipping) (3x)
A boy and girl came skipping,
There's lots of work to do.

This is the way we (rake the ground) (3x) **R**
This is the way we rake the ground,
In our Springtime garden. **SP**

Rick, rack, rake, **R**
All the lumps must break,
Here we go, to and fro,
Rick, rack, rake.

Hack, (3x) Hack my little hoe, **K**
Weeds, (3x) All the weeds must go. **G**

This is the way we dig the ground, etc. **G**

This is the way we plant the seeds, etc. **S**
(put feet together to say the magic verse)

"Father Sun, shine on our seeds and make them grow. **A O**
Sister Rain, rain on our seeds and make them grow. **R O**
Brother Wind, blow on our seeds and make them grow." **W O**

This is the way the sun does shine, etc. **A**

This is the way the rain falls down, etc. **R**

This is the way the wind does blow, etc. **W**

This is the way the butterflies fly, etc. **L**

Bring in: caterpillars creep, beetles crawl, snails do slide…(anything that lives in the garden). Pull the weeds, spiders spin, fairies fly, grasshoppers spring, squirrels run, etc.

This is the way the flowers grow, etc.
This is the way the flowers die, etc.
This is the way the new ones grow, etc.

Growing verse for leaves:

(4x) **L** from small to big, the **O** as bud and slowly open bud. When opening the bud it is important to imagine the flower unfolding as the children can "latch onto" this.

Live again, leaf again, love again, life again.
All aglow.

8

In our springtime garden,
Sunlight all aglow,
Breezes blowing, blowing, blowing,
Lovely grass does grow.

In our springtime garden,
Precious stones do glow,
Little dwarfie sits and listens,
Bunny jumps just so.

In the bright laughing dew,
So we dance, I and you,
Like the stars in the sky,
So we dance, you and I.
And the leaves in the trees
Do delight us and please,
And the wind in the grass
Sings a song as we pass.

9

There in the woods I see a tree,
The loveliest tree you ever could see,
And the green leaves grew around, around, around,
And the green leaves grew around.
There in the tree I see a nest,
The loveliest nest you ever did see,
And the green leaves...around.
There in the nest I see four eggs,
The loveliest eggs you ever could see,
And the green leaves...around
Then from the eggs I see four birds,
The loveliest birds you ever did see
And the green leaves...around.

10

Waken sleeping butterfly, burst your narrow prison,
Spread your golden wings and fly, for the sun is risen,
Spread your wings and tell the story,
How He rose, the King of glory.

One child crouches right down in the center of the ring holding a yellow/gold silk or muslin cloth by the two corners. The cloth covers the child. At "burst," the child starts slowly to unfold, then flies around. If the cloth is silk, then it is an added pleasure for the child to have the cloth over the head as well while flying, as the "world" then is seen through a golden glow.

Caterpillar wind about,
Round and round and in and out,
When you are fed, spin your bed,
Go to sleep, deep, deep,
As a caterpillar die,
Waken as a butterfly.
Rise from death and unfold,
Spread your soft wings of gold,
Upward fly to the light,
Bringing joy and delight.

Nest Building ☙

(capitals = large movements, small = small movements, e.g. **A, a**.)

Mummy Bird and Daddy Bird loved each other true, **A b D b O u**
Said Mummy Bird to Daddy Bird, **A b D b**
"Build a nest, please do. **e D**
Build it straight and build it strong, **T t shoulders**
And build it on a branch thaaaat long." **B e out sideways**
Daddy Bird went flying. **L around circle**
There was a tall, tall tree **T** *and under the tree was a river,*
V *and in the river there were f-f-fishes.*
And the f-f-fishes swam in, and the f-f-fishes swam out **f f fingers**
"Here I will build a nest," he said, "And then when our baby birds come out of their eggs they will be able to look down and watch the fishes swimming."
"Fetch some twigs, weave them in. (bend or turn to fetch twigs **V**)
Fetch some leaves, weave them in.

11

Weave and weave and weave a nest,
Weave a nest for me,
Weave and weave and weave a nest,
Weave it in the tree (weave one hand/arm at a time **V**),
(call) *Mummy Bird, Mummy Bird,* **A b A b**
Come and see your nest!" **e**

Mummy bird came flying **L**
She shook it, **sh** *and she poked it,* **p** *and she said, "No!"* **(negation)**
"Silly Daddy Bird, what happens if Brother Wind comes and gives a big blow? **W**
Then my nest will go round and round and round **r r** *and splash* **sh** *into the water and my*
baby birds will drown dead. **D down**
Build another nest,
Build it straight, and build it strong,
And build it on a branch thaaat long."

"I'm tired," said Daddy Bird, "but, yes, (foot) *I will do it,*
Because I love you!" **O**
Daddy Bird went flying.
(can sing while flying)

12

"Fly, Daddy Bird, fly,
Fly through the sky
Flying over hill and dale,
Flying over mountain vale,
Fly, Daddy Bird, fly. Fly through the sky."

There he saw such a big tree **T***, and it had a branch low down, and under the branch was*
some soft grass. **s**
"Here I will build a nest," **e** *he said, "so that if our babies fall out of their nest, they won't*
hurt themselves."
"Fetch some twigs, weave them in (as before), *and she poked it, and she said, "No!"*
"Silly Daddy Bird, didn't you see that cat? **K t to shoulders** *He will sit on the branch and*
wait **e** *and then he will grab* **r b** *my little birds and eat them up.* **t to mouth** *No!*
Build another nest,
Build it straight, and build it strong,
And build it on a branch thaaat long."

"Oh" said Daddy Bird, "I am tired,
But, yes, I will do it, because I love you!"

And away Daddy Bird flew.
(sing: Fly, Daddy Bird, Fly as before)

There below he saw a tree **T***, and in the tree there was a bush* **B** *and in the bush there was a hole* **o***. "Here I will build a nest," he said "Here our little birds will be quite safe."*

"Fetch some leaves, weave them in.
Fetch some twigs, weave them in.
Fetch some bits of wool, weave them in (or grass, etc.).
(sing) "Weave and weave (as before, this time also both hands/arms).
"Mummy Bird...poked it, and she said, "Yes!" (foot)

"Wait!" said Daddy Bird, and he pulled out his softest feathers from over his heart and he put it down **d** *in the nest. "Now you can sit!" (all sit)*
And she sat, and she laid two little eggs (all sit with fists together)..
And the sun went up, and the sun went down **A up and down***, and she sat.*
And the moon went up and the moon went down **U** *and she sat.*
And the stars went up and the stars went down, **A** *and she sat. (arms up and down each time, then back into fists)*

And one morning, when the sun came up, "Cheep!" out came a little birdie (pointer finger **l** *from right hand). "Tweetyweeee!" which means "I'm hungry!" Give him a worm to eat (lips to finger). Let him fly (out a little, back to nest, gradually out more and more until full arm stretch with fingers fluttering and back to nest each time; contraction and expansion).*

Next morning "Cheep!" Out came little brother. "Tweetyweee!" (repeat)

"Let's fly together," they said (contraction and expansion from small to big and back silently).

They looked out of their nest **u with both pointers** *and there they saw a little house (describe the school) and out of the house came 1, 2, 3...(count the children). "How can there be so many children with one Mummy," they said. And then they saw a lady come out and call "Storytime, children." "It's a Kindergarten! Teetywee, tweetywee, tweetywee,"* *they called.* **i pointer fingers**

"Look!" cried the children, "There are two little birds. We must put crumbs out for them."

"We can fly! You can't fly!" called the little birds. **L with hands**

"We can do lots that you can't do," said the children. (stand)

"We can go on tip, tip toe, like the fairies we can go,
We can go, so you would say, an elephant in on his way (stamp),
We can ruuun, and we can hop,
And we can spin just like a top **T**
And we can put our arms far and wide, and we can sway from side to side."

(See-saw, Marjorie Daw, or other sway song, briefly)

"We can make ourselves so tall,
And we can make ourselves so small,
We can kneel without a sound,
And sit cross-legged on the ground,
And stand like candles on a birthday cake."

This story the children have loved year after year. It can be done in sections and the last part can be left out if necessary. The children identify with the two birds and want to leave crumbs out in the garden for them. To get a birdbath is a good follow-up. I have had no problem with doing the whole story with four- to six-year-olds and a shortened version for three-year-olds.

The Flower Queen ✿

The Flower Queen had golden shoes
She put them on her feet
With every step the flowers grew
They smelled so fresh and sweet. (soft walking, feeling the soles of the feet)

A dragon (or witch) came a (creeping by) (3x) **R**
The Flower Queen to take (all creep like a dragon or witch, then the teacher grabs one child and puts her in the center and builds a tower around her out of about five children who hold hands facing outwards)
He (she) put her in a (tower tall) (3x)
And closed it firm and strong.

Maybe the water can wash the stones away? (other children become the river and go around the tower with **V**)
And all around the (water wept) (3x) (stand with **W** from side to side)
The Flower Queen is gone **G**

Maybe the birds can fly over the tower and pull her out?
And all around the (birds did fly) (3x) (fly with **L** around the tower)
The Flower Queen is gone (**G** with big wings)

Maybe the fire can burn the tower down
And then the fire (flickered high) (3x) **F F from down upwards**
The Flower Queen is gone. **G**

Then came the Sun Prince brave and bold **e B**
With eyes of blue and cloak of gold **U O**
(all the outside children then do as teacher)
Come my sunbeams, come to me **M**
Today we set the Flower Queen free! **F**
There is a dark dragon before the gate, **DR**
Wicked he is and full of hate, **K h in**
But come my sunbeams, never fear, **M**
That wicked dragon we'll chase from here. **K CH**

"Go (3x) Dragon (witch) you must go! **G**
Or we will prick you, we will stick you, we will race you, we will chase you! **i i R CH**
Go (3x) dragon you must go!" **G**
(outer children run around the tower with **i** as spears—they love this. On "Go!" they stamp the four steps with **G**)

The dragon is gone, **G**
Oh dwarfs come here
And break the rocks **K**
The path to make clear.

(outer children become dwarfs and do the verse)
We hammer, hammer ding, dang, dong (fists on fists)
We dig and dig with axes strong,
With nick and nack now lift the sack
With clip and clap go pick-a-back,
Over to the tower!

13

Here we are the clever little mountain gnomes (march around tower)
And we have now left our mountain homes
With our little hammers bright
We will knock with all our might
For we want to set our Flower Queen free.
Knock (3x) you must come with me! (free one "stone" at a time—that stone becomes a dwarf and follows)
Last time: Now the Flower Queen is free.

14

All: *Wake up, wake up the sun shines bright*
The dark is conquered by the light.
And all the flowers under the ground are slowly beginning to grow.
Live again, leaf again, love again, life again, all aglow. (growing L's)
And the prince of the sun and the sunbeams came down to dance with the Flower Queen.
(they dance together and all the others dance in a ring around them)

The Little White Butterfly

Once upon a time there was a little caterpillar. He was creeping and creeping and creeping **r**, *and eating and eating and eating* **t to mouth**, *and he got fatter and fatter and fatter* **f 2x out to side**, *and he sang:*

15

"I'm a big fat caterpillar eating all day **B t to mouth**
Munch, munch, munch, in a funny kind of way. **m by mouth**
I eat all day and I eat all night, **t**
I eat so much that my skin feels tight." **t**
And as he grew fatter and fatter and fatter **F**, *he grew sleepier and sleepier and sleepier* **P**, *so he spun himself a little house.* **P** *turning around, and went fast asleep.* (long pause, with arms folded across chest)

And the sun went up, and the sun went down. **A up and down**, *and he slept.*
And the moon went up, and the moon went down. **U** *And he slept.*
And the stars went up and the stars went down, **A** *and he slept.*
And he wriggled a little **r shoulder**, *and he slept.*
One morning a sunbeam woke him,

14

"Wake up, wake up, the sun shines bright, **e a**
* The dark is conquered by the light."* **d k l** (can repeat with arms and legs)
* He opened his eyes, and he stretched, and whoops! A wing!* **P**
* And whoops! Another wing!* **P**
"I'm a butterfly! I'm a butterfly!" he shouted. **L**

12

"Fly, butterfly, fly,
* Fly through the sky*
* Flying over hill and dale,*
* Flying over mountain vale*
* Fly, butterfly, fly,*
* Flying through the sky."*

And he flew to a stone by a little pond **O**. *There he sat.* **e** *He put his wings up* **high.**
He put his wings down **low,** *and he looked into the water.* **u**
"Oh no! Oh no! My wings are white! I don't want white wings! **Neg. W**
*I know. The grass is green. If I rub my wings in the grass, the green of the grass will rub off
onto my wings, and my wings will be green!"*

So he rubbed his wings this way, and he rubbed his wings that way, (repeat). **R**
*Back to the stone flew the little butterfly. There he sat. He put his wings up high. He put his
wings down low, and he looked into the water.*
"Oh no! Oh no! My wings are still white!"

He looked up at the sky. "The sky is blue," **U** *he said, "If I fly through the blue sky my wings
will become blue like the sky!" and off he flew. (repeat verse/song)*

*Back to the stone flew the little butterfly. There he sat. He put his wings up high. He put his
wings down low, and looked into the water. "Oh no! Oh no! My wings are still white!"
There above him was a rainbow.* **O** *"I know," he said, "I will fly in and out of all the colors
and I'll be a rainbow butterfly!" Off he flew again.*

"Fly, butterfly, fly, fly through the rainbow **L**
Fly through the red, fly through the orange, fly through the yellow
Fly through the green, fly through the blue, fly through the purple
Fly through the violet." (can do the colors, but not necessary)

*Back to the stone flew the little butterfly. He put his wings up high. He put his wings down
low. He looked into the water. "Oh no! Oh no!' he cried "My wings are still white!"*

He flew to a little yellow daisy, sat on her petals and gave a big **sigh** **h down with shoul-**
ders *and wept.* **wp** *"Why do you cry, little butterfly?" asked the yellow daisy.* **Ei ei ei**
"I am weeping because my wings are white," he wept. **w w w**
The daisy felt so sorry for the little butterfly that two tears like dewdrops went down, down
its petals and dropped onto the butterfly's wings. **t from eyes into d down**

The butterfly flew to a little blue daisy. (repeat above)
The butterfly flew to a red rose. (repeat)
The butterfly flew back to the stone. "I'm going to throw myself into the water and drown,"
he said. **D down**

Just then he heard, "Kwaak, kwaaak!" and there, sitting by the stone was a big frog. **G**
"What is the matter that you look so sad?" asked the frog. **?**
"I don't want to have white wings!" wept the butterfly.
"But you don't have white wings!" said the frog. **Neg**

The little butterfly looked into the water **U**. *Where the yellow tears* **t** *of the yellow daisy had*
fallen **f down** *were yellow spots, and where the blue tears of the blue daisy had fallen there*
were blue spots, and where the red tears from the red rose had fallen there were red spots!

"Hooray!" **H jump** *he shouted, "I'm spotty!* **P jump** *I'm spotty! I'm a spotty butterfly! I'm*
the only spotty butterfly in the whole wide world." Away he flew.

Fly, spotty butterfly, fly (same verse/song)

Additional ending which the children love:

The children can fly freely around the room, bearing in mind that butterflies have
such delicate wings that they never ever touch each other. When the teacher plays a
chord or claps hands, the children have to fly back to the circle.

Note:
If the children need to be "anchored" during the story, a beetle with a definite walking rhythm or a dwarf or grasshopper can also ask the butterfly why he cries. They
then answer, *"Poor thing!"* and go on.

AUTUMN

The Autumn leaves are (falling down) (3x) **F down**
The Autumn leaves are falling down
Ooooo, the wind blows through. **U**

(Or: depending on the weather, The Autumn rains are raining down, etc.) **R**

"I'm cold (wet), I'm cold (wet)," said the little bear, (2x) **K (W) B**
"I go to Mother Earth's cave." (bear walk) **B arms and legs**
He came to the door of the caves.
"Knock, knock, knock, little door unlock." **(K** or stamp, clap, etc.)

A little dwarf opened the door, and they went down, down, down into a cave where it was snuggly warm. **D d d d down s m**

The dwarf covered him with leaves, and he fell fast asleep. **V L**
(snores—do contraction and expansion with arms in and out)

Repeat: *The Autumn leaves are falling down...*
"I'm cold, I'm cold," said the little mouse (2x) **k m** (use fingers)
"I go to Mother Earth's cave." (mouse-steps on tip-toe)

Repeat as above but in miniature.

Repeat the above pattern with any animal (children can also suggest) with movements to match the animal, e.g. tortoise, rabbit, great, big bear, etc.

When a large animal (e.g. elephant) wants to enter, then, of course, he will get stuck, so the dwarfs have to make the cave bigger:

"Hammer (3x), knock (3x)" repeated many times, hammering one fist on the other, up and down, turning, etc. Then sweep the stones out of the doorway.

This is the way we (sweep the stones) (3x) (repeat)
Sweep them out of the door. **(S** from center circle backwards to perimeter)

They all snore in different ways. The rabbit can snore with his ears doing contraction and expansion, mouse with hands doing same.

All was quiet, and all the dwarfs sang softly (sitting and cradling arms)

16

"Go to sleep now, little animals, night is coming blue and deep,
Stars are bright and angels carry, down from heaven holy sleep,
Aa-a-ai-ah, (2x) down from heaven holy sleep."

Each lesson can repeat animals or have new ones, e.g. a lion can come, but the dwarfs have to make a special cave for him because the other animals might be frightened.

Further ideas:
One could also have:
Little bird...fly into my nest
Tiny mouse...tiny house
Little cat...go to the fire on my cosy mat...

If it rains, one can start with the "Raining" (see **Weather Verses**, page 97.)

Always do few sounds but descriptive and "filled."

The Golden Apples ❀

Once upon a time there was a King. He had a very beautiful daughter but she was so ill that he thought, "Surely she will **die.**" **D** *So, he called out throughout the land, "Who, oh who, will make her better?* **U e (ay) e** *Who, oh who, will make her better?" But no one came.* **negation**

So he called his wise men to him. There was one who had a beard **B** *down to here and he walked like this.* **soul-gesture knowledge** *He came into the room, looked at the princess* **U** *and said "No, I cannot make her better."* **negation**

The King called out again, "Who, oh who... (2x)" There came a second wise man who had a beard down to here, and who walked like this: **solemnity** *He, too, looked at the princess and said, "No, I cannot make her better* **negation**

Again the King called out: "Who, oh who... (2x)"
Along came a third wise man, who had a beard down to here (even lower). *He walked like this* **inwardness** *He looked at the princess and he said:*
"Yes! **foot affirmative**
A golden apple I can see, **O**
That is what will set her free!" **a F**

The King called: "Who, oh who, will bring to me **U B**
A golden apple from the tree?" **O T**

Along came a whole lot of little children (skipping). "We will get it," they said. But where were they to find it? **?** "I know," said one "The King of the gnomes lives under the ground, **O D down**. He surely knows all the trees in the world. **L** Let us ask him."

There were the Dwarfs doing their hammering (one fist beats on the other).
"*Hammer*, (3x) *knock* (3x) (pause, then each time louder)
"*Hammer*, (3x) *knock* (3x) (pause, continue letting them join in the words each time louder, also stamping feet, until they even scream, then catch them with:

"*Take out your golden hammer*." (2 fingers of the right hand and tap the left fist)
(softly) "*Hammer*," etc.

Now take out your silver hammer (one finger—higher, softer voice)
"*Hammer* (3x) *knock* (3x) *Silver shining golden bright*
Brighter than the moon at night." (long-short rhythm).

The children put their feet together and said:
"*Dwarfie*, (2x) *under the ground*, **Dff n D down**
Have you a golden apple found?" **U O**
"No." **neg.** *he said*, "You had better ask the King of the squirrels, he knows all the trees." **L**
(T)

There was the king of the squirrels (run and jump, but this is not necessary)
"*What's your hurrrrry mister squirrel* **Rrrr**
With your tail up in a whirrrl.
Do you have to rrrush and scamperrrr
Just because you are a squirrrel?
(clap) *1, 2, 3, 4, we have many nuts to store*
(clap) *5, 6, 7, 8, hide them quick before it's late*." (repeat these two lines alternating fast and slow. Do "store" **O** in front and "hide" **H** behind back.

The children put their feet together:
"*Squirrel* (2x) *in the tree*, **Rrr T**
Have you a golden apple for me?" **U O**
"No." *said the King of the squirrels*, "Ask the King of the eagles, he can see all the trees in the whole world." **L**

The King of the eagles was flying.

12
"Fly, eagle, fly, fly through the sky,
Flying over hill and dale,
Flying over mountain vale
Fly, eagle, fly, fly through the sky"

Fly with big wings **L**. Can straighten wings and dip them towards center when coming to land.

*He had sharp claws **k** and a sharp beak b so the children quickly put their feet together and said:*
"Eagle (2x) in the air, **L L R**
Have you a golden apple there?" **U O**

"No." (big wing **negation** movement)

Now, what are we going to do? No golden apple-tree anywhere. Let's think. **knowledge**
I know! There must be a golden apple-tree in heaven. Let's go and see. But how do we get there? (ask children) Over the rainbow!

But first we have to make our feet soft. Imagine what would happen if you rubbed some of the colors off? Or if you slipped and fell through?
Point and point and point your toes,
Point them softly, point them so.
Now we point from side to side,
Point them softly, not too wide.
Now we're going to point behind
Point them gently, make them kind.
Now, we're going to cross our feet
Cross them over, nice and neat.
Now roll your foot (first one, then the other, then both)
Now hold hands so that you won't get lost.

1

Here we go, on tip-toe, over the rainbow bridge we go,
Walking softly, walking slow, over the rainbow bridge we go.
Up into the heavens far, gathering light from sun and star,
Down to earth all things to greet, bringing light to all we meet.

With the above verse/song, lead the children into the "magic spiral" and out so that they have turned "inside-out" and have their backs facing the center of the circle. Jump around to face circle center.

There stands a big apple-tree **T**
Stand fast at root, bear well at top. **U T**
Every little twig, bears an apple big. **l (little finger) B**
Every little bough bears an apple now, and they are golden!" **b O**

17

Shake, shake the apple tree, apples that are golden (2x) **Sh k (2) T O**
One for you, one for me, shake (2x) the apple-tree. **U M(in) Sh k (2) T**
Put only one apple in your pocket. Hold hands (the whole process home is reversed)

The children came to the castle. They came into the princess' room. There she lay on the bed. She was hardly breathing. (stand eyes closed)

The children cut the apple into pieces (little cutting-movements **k**).
They put a little piece into the princess' mouth, and her eyes went open.
They put another piece into her mouth, and she sat up in bed **e**
They put another piece in her mouth, and she jumped out of bed, **P** *and she said, "I'm bet-ter, I'm better, I'm very, very better!"* Repeat and jump with alternate feet crossing and hands crossing in **e (ay)**.

The king was so happy he had a big cake made, and he gave each child a big piece.

Note:
This story can be extended over at least four weeks. The cooks at the castle can even bake the cake for the children. Putting in flour, sugar, etc. and mixing. It can also be done in sections, then repeating parts and going further, etc. or even completely from beginning to end.

29

Autumn Leaves

The autumn leaves are falling down,
Gold and red and russet brown,
In the countryside and in the town,
They're falling all the day.
We're kicking through the autumn leaves,
The lovely autumn tinted leaves,
The oak, the beech, the chestnut leaves,
We're kicking the leaves away.
We're sweeping up the autumn leaves,
The lovely autumn tinted leaves,
The oak, the beech and the chestnut leaves,
We're sweeping the leaves away.
The leaves are piling higher and higher,
We'll make a lovely autumn fire,
The flames are burning higher and higher,
We'll burn the leaves away.

Little Leaves Fall Gently Down

Little leaves fall gently down
Red and yellow, orange and brown
Whirling, whirling round and round
Quietly, without a sound
Falling softly to the ground
Down and down and down
S s s ssschh.

Over Branches Without a Rest

Over branches without a rest,
Runs the squirrel to his nest
Gathering acorns every day
Safe for winter stored away.

WHISKY, FRISKY

Whisky, frisky, hippity hop
Up he goes to the tree top.
Whirly, twirly, round and round
Down he scampers to the ground.
Furly, curly, what a tail
Tall as a feather, broad as a sail.
Where's his supper? In the shell.
Snappety, crackity out it fell.

WHAT'S YOUR HURRY, MR. SQUIRREL?

What's your hurry, Mr. Squirrel?
With your tail up in a whirrrrl.
Do you have to rrrush and scamperrr,
Just because your name is squirrel?
1, 2, 3, 4, we have many nuts to store
5, 6, 7, 8, hide them quick, before it's late.

Because the **R** belongs so much to the squirrel, it can be exaggerated and rolled on the tongue. The children love imitating the sound and it is very healthy for them to do so as it makes the tongue active. For the last two lines of the verse, the children can clap the first four numbers then an **O** in front, then clap the last four and **H** to behind the back. This can be repeated with speeding up and slowing down and with feet and fingers.

MICHAELMAS ✿

There was once a Prince. He was strong **T to shoulders** *and brave* **B** *with a* **h***eart of gold,*
O *and he was a helper of the great angel, Michael.* **E (ay) up as wings**
One morning, a sunbeam shone through his window:

14

Wake up, wake up, the sun shines bright **e A eA A** *(all done with arms plus legs)*
The dark is conquered by the light. **D K L**
He put on his clothes. He put on his golden cloak **O***, fastened it with a golden brooch* **o***. He*
put on his golden crown **O** *and his walking boots* **U** *and did his verse to make him strong.*
"I am strong, I am brave, I am valiant and bold,
For the sun fills my heart with his life-giving gold.
I am helpful and truthful and loving and free
For the sun's golden rays do shine brightly in me."

The children cannot be expected to step a rhythm in kindergarten. A descriptive
vowel or consonant on every long beat is sufficient.

Off he went into the forest to look for helpers for the angel, Michael.
As he walked so straight and strong *(walk upright)*
A sly old fox came trotting along (descriptive movements).
"May I be a helper too? **e e u**
Tell me what I ought to do." **e o d**

"You must be brave, you must be bold, (very upright) **E B**
Tell the truth, and have a heart of gold." **u A O**

Do you think he can be a helper, children? (go into the merits of the fox) *No.*

As he stood there straight and strong, a big brown bear came walking along.
"I'm a big, brown, bristly, bushy bear **B** *(walk)*
I rumble and tumble through bush and through bramble,
I'm a big, brown, bristly, bushy bear."

The bear stopped and said, "May I be a helper too? (same as above but as bear)
Tell me what I ought to do."

"You must be brave, you must be bold,
Tell the truth, and have a heart of gold."

Again discuss the merits of the bear with the children and decide.

And as he stood there, straight and strong, a great big eagle came flying along. **L**
(discuss again, eagle can see far, can see the dragon, etc.)

Others to come in the same way: bee, snake, etc. The last can be a horse. The horse can become the prince's horse, but must first go to horse-training school, as described elsewhere. The horse-training school is the children's favorite (see page 102).

Another Michaelic verse is:

To slay the foe, with strength we go,
We wield with might, our sword of light.
To right the wrong, we battle strong,
Our deeds are bold, and shine like gold.

The above story works well as a plan for the following, or the one can work to eventually follow the other. Use the same theme and even the same beginning but with a king instead of a prince.

"King, King, with your eyes so blue, **K U** (done to suit the animal)
May I be a King one day like you?" **E K D U**
"My hands, heart, head, they work for all, **hE hA hd L**
I do not have your claws at all." (or teeth, whiskers, tail, trunk, etc. depending on which animal approaches)

WINTER

Deep in the earth, all is quiet and the animals are fast asleep and snoring. (all sit)

Do contraction and expansion with arms while making one snore breath in—arms expanded, one snore breath out—arms contracted. The rabbit can snore with hands on either side of head as ears contracting and expanding, the mouse using fingers only, tortoise with head going up and down slowly, etc.

The dwarfs were singing softly "Aa-a-aia-aa-a-aia." **Al**

"I wonder what they are dreaming," said a dwarf, "Let's do magic and find out. (standing)
Deep, deep, in winter's sleep, lay a little rabbit **D down b**
Dream, dream, what do you dream?" **M**

*"What do I dream?" said the rabbit. "I dream that I am hopping, a-hopping, a-hopping, I
dream that I'm a-hopping, in the summer sun."* **P A**
(hop to music or "Hop, little bunny, hop, little bunny, hop, little bunny, hop, hop, hop."
"And I dream that I am eating carrots (make bunny-teeth and bite over bottom lip) *in
the summer sun."* **A**

Let's find out what the beetle is dreaming.
"Deep, deep, in winter's sleep, lay a little beetle, **D B**
Dream, dream, what do you dream?" **M**

"I dream that I'm a-grabbeling, (3x)
I dream that I'm a-grabbeling, in the summer sun." (do beetle walk **B**) **A**

"Deep... bear. Dream... dream?" **D B M**

"I dream that I am walking through the forest:
I'm a baby, brown, bristly, bushy bear, **b**
I rumble and tumble through bush and through bramble
I'm a baby, brown, bristly, bushy bear (bear **b** walk)
And I dream that I smell honey (sniff, sniff) *and there's a beehive at the top of the tree and
I climb the tree* (**B**'s) *and I blow the bees away* (blow) *and I put my paw inside the beehive,
and take out the honey and taste it. Mmmmm, and the other paw, Mmmm* (alternate
paws until they do nice **M**'s). *Then I mix some honey for the dwarfs* **M** *and go down the
tree."* **B**

Deep... lay a little ladybird
Dream... dream?
"I dream that I am flying (3x)... sun." (fly with **L A**)

Deep... caterpillar. Dream... dream?
"What am I dreaming?" said the caterpillar?
"I dream that I am eating, and eating, and eating. **T to mouth**

15

I'm a big fat caterpillar eating all day **B T to mouth**
Munch, munch, munch in a funny kind of way, **M**
I eat all day and I eat all night, **T**
I eat so much that my skin feels tight, **T**
And then I yawn, and I yawn, **Y** or **O**
And I spin a little house around me, and go to sleep (pause). **P** *turn and contract*
Then I make a little hole in the top of my house,
And I stretch, and whoops! Out pops a wing **WP**
And whoops! Out pops another wing **WP**
And I dream that I am a butterfly!" **L**

12

Fly, butterfly, fly, fly through the sky,
Flying over hill and dale
Flying over mountain vale,
Fly, butterfly, fly, fly through the sky."

The above format and repetition can be used for other animals, etc. The children can also suggest and the teacher decides how to take it up.

"Sh, sh." said the dwarfs." sleep now (2x) **Ssh**

16

"Go to sleep now, little darlings, (cradle arms)
Night is coming blue and deep,
Stars are bright and angels carry,
Down from heaven holy sleep,
A-a-aiya (2x), Down from heaven holy sleep."

THE ANGELS/ADVENT

Now children, you know how busy we all are getting ready for Christmas, but do you know who are even busier? The angels!

When baby Jesus is born they have to fly all over the earth to tell all the animals and the plants and the insects. "Baby Jesus is born," (2x) and sometimes their wings can get tired, so they have to practice with their wings.

First of all, get them nice and loose. Round and round r r r r r **R with shoulders, backwards then forwards**

"Fly, angels, fly, fly through the sky." (sing or music) *(Fly with* **L** *in circle)*
Now we may have to fly to tell an elephant, then quickly turn to fly to a lion, then quickly turn to fly to a monkey, so we have to learn to turn without touching wings. You know that birds fly without touching? Well, angels also never touch wings. Now fly, and when you hear me clap then turn quickly and fly the other way (music or sing).

That was good, but we will have to practice that again next time.

When baby Jesus is born, we will also have to go up and down the heavenly ladders. They are shiny gold, and it would be terrible if we slip, so we had better make our feet nice and soft:
"Point and point and point your toe (alternate feet).
Point them softly, point them so.
Now we point from side to side, (feet together neatly between side points)
Point them softly not too wide.
Now we're going to cross our feet,
Cross them softly, cross them neat,
Now we're going to point behind
Point them gently, make them kind.
Now roll your foot." (first one, then the other, then both)
(can also walk on toes, then heels)

Next we have to practice bell-ringing, because when the baby is born all the bells on earth are ringing.
First, the golden bells (hands together and ring from side to side)
"Ring, glocklein, ting-a-ling-a-ling, (high voice)
Ring, glocklein, ring." (2x)

Now the silver bells (arms apart and swing to center and away again)
"Ring, silver bells, ring-a-ling-a-ling, (middle voice)
Ring, silver bells, ring." (2x)
Now the church bells (feet apart, hands joined and swing between feet down and up)
"Ring, church bells, ring-a-ling-a-ling, (low voice)
Ring, church bells, ring." (2x)

The above can be played on chime-bars, etc. high medium and low, and then the children on their own listen and do what they hear.

Now we also have to grow lilies for the Angel Gabriel to take to Mary (Mulberry Bush tune):
"This is the way we (dig the clouds) (3x)
To grow a lily for Christmas."

"Put in the seed, cover it with cloud, say the magic verse, **s v**
Father Sun, shine on our lilies and make them grow, **a o**
Sister Rain, rain on our lilies and make them grow, **r o**
Brother Wind, blow on our lilies and make them grow." **w o**

Then all sit down, let the children watch while you grow a lily, making two leaves at a time grow from the bottom of the stem, each time higher (2x), then the bud—up the stem, then open the bud. As the children imitate what the teacher "sees," it must be done with inner visualization.

All together:
Live again, Leaf again, Life again, Love again, All aglow (bud)
(all open buds silently with reverence)
Leave it there for the Angel Gabriel.

The following is done at the last lesson before Christmas. Put a candle in one end of a short copper rod. Put silver foil around the bottom of the candle in the shape of a rose to prevent painful drips. Close the curtains.

Tell the children that when the Christ Child came to be born, he brought with him a heavenly light to light his way. This he planted deep into the earth to make the earth shine. This little light has to go on a heavenly journey, and so has to practice to become strong. He whispers to the teacher in a dream to tell the children that he is coming and please to make something for him to journey on.

Then take the copper rod, light a match but focus full concentration on the wick. The flame on the match is merely a vehicle for "little light." As the candle flame flares up say, "Hello, little light," and talk to it, it will take on a personality and will flicker in excitement when in contact with the breath. Pass it around the circle. Each child must hold the rod with both hands as he takes it and passes to the next. When it has completed the circle, then pass it around the other way. Then hold it and do a small circle and pass it on. Finally the teacher can slowly in **S** form raise the rod high and bring it down. Then all say goodbye to "little light" and the teacher blows the flame out and follows it invisibly going up. All this time the teacher either hums a tune or sings *Over Stars Is Mary Wandering,* or there can be lyre, etc.

Any of these sections can be done in circle time by the kindergarten teacher.

One can also create a heavenly ladder or rainbow, by putting copper rods or silk scarves at "stepping" intervals on the floor. With the teacher demonstrating first, the children copy one at a time: stepping over, hopping over with both feet, hopping on one leg (with help) over the rods/colors.

Verse to end (hands in prayer position):

Gentle Jesus, meek and mild, look upon this little child,
Make me gentle as thou art, come and live within my heart.
Take these child-like hands in thine, guide these little feet of mine.
So may all my happy days, sing your joyous song of praise,
And the world will always see, Christ, the Holy Child in me. Amen.

This verse is best used for the last or last two lessons only.

Additions:

One can also have the Angels washing their dresses (*Mulberry Bush* tune):

This is the way we wash the dress...to get it ready for Christmas.
Wring *the dress,* **H**ang *the dress (on the rainbow)* **I**ron, **fo**ld, etc.

One can also sew a new white silk dress for when the baby is born. Round stitches with gold thread and "up-and-down" stitches with silver thread.

A simple tune to accompany:

Round and round and round we sew,
Sewing, sewing, sewing, sew.
Up (high note) *and down* (low note)

The following lesson "lit" into me when doing the **Big Blue Boat** (see page 56). The children were busy with Advent stories and had just had the story about Mary. As they were lining up to enter the room the story "happened" and then created itself as the lesson continued. It turned out to be blessed with a wonderful mood. It can be used either as the boat for Mary's birth or for Baby Jesus' birth.

19
The Golden Boat (Blue Boat)

And Mary (Baby Jesus) came down in a golden boat, a golden boat...etc. **B** (round the circle)
The golden boat it had two white sails...on the golden boat. **U into L**
The golden boat had a golden flag...a flag right on the top. **F**
And all the angels were flying around...around the golden boat. **L B**
And look at the stars how they twinkled down...down to the earth below. **A D**
And even the moon sent her moonbeams down...down on the golden boat.
And soft white doves see them flutter around...flutter around the boat **S B**
A beautiful rainbow it covered the sky...around the golden boat. **O Ei**
And see the boat how it floated down...floated right down to the earth **F down**
And look a mother was waiting there...waiting for her child **rev. E**
And then Mother Mary (Baby Jesus) was born on the earth...was born down on the earth **B**
And look how the mother now rocked her Child...rocked her Mary (Jesus) Child (cradle arms)

Summer and "Fill-In" Stories

Milk Bottle Story

Once upon a time, long, long ago, there lived a farmer who kept lots of cows and goats in a field. Every day he milked them. (milking song with mainly **m**, e.g. *"Moo, moo, milk cow, milk so moist and yummy. Moo, moo, milk cow milk now for my tummy."*) To milk, bend at right angles forward from the waist with feet apart and do **M** from tummy to the floor.

One day, when he had finished milking all the cows and goats, the biggest milk bottle fell from the farmer's house, bump, bump, bump and bump **B** (repeat) *and rolled into the field.* **R**

Along that way came Mr. Mouse. (if no music, then, *"Tip-toe, tip-toe, little mousie, Tip-toe, tip-toe, where's your housie."*)

"Here is a house, a pretty little house. **Small h out, small h in**

Who lives in this house?" **?**

"Now me, Mr. Mouse." **i m**

And along that way, where the milk bottle fell, **f** *down came Mr. Hare.* (Hop Mr. Rabbit, hop Mr. Rabbit, hop Mr. Rabbit, hop, hop, hop.) **ears up**

"Here is a house, a pretty little house. Who lives in this house?"

"Me, Mr. Mouse, and who are you?" **i m m u a u ?**

"I am Mr. Hare. May I come in?" **small sounds with ears e a n**

And along that way, where the milk bottle fell, came Mr. Fox. (Fox, fox, sniffling through the wood, fox, fox, sniffing for some food.) **f arms straight in front**

"Here is a house, a pretty little house. Who lives in this house?"
"Me, Mr. Mouse." "Me, Mr. Hare." "And who are you?"
"I am Mr. Fox. May I come in?"
"Well, come in."

And along that way, where the milk bottle fell, came Mr. Wolf. **W F**
"Here is a house, a pretty little house. Who lives in this house?"
"Me, Mr. Mouse." "Me, Mr. Hare." "Me, Mr. Fox." "And who are you?"
"I am Mr. Wolf. May I come in?"
"Well, come in."

And along the way, where the milk bottle fell, came Mr. Bear.
"I'm a big, brown, bristly, bushy bear. I rumble and tumble through bush and through
  bramble. I'm a big, brown, bristly, bushy bear." **B** (bear walk)
"Here is a house, a pretty little house. Who lives in this house?"
"Me, Mr. Mouse." "Me, Mr. Hare." "Me, Mr. Fox." "Me, Mr. Wolf." "And who are you?"
"I am Mr. Bear. May I come in?"
"No, no, no. You are too fat!"
"I am too fat? I'll smash you all flat!"

But, no matter how hard he tried, the milk bottle was too strong, so off he went!
And Mr. Mouse, and Mr. Hare, and Mr. Fox, and Mr. Wolf all laughed and laughed then
crept inside the milk bottle and went fast asleep.

The sounds must be done to suit the animals.

Baking Day
Created by a Eurythmy student

It was very early in the morning when the sun began to peep over the mountain.
It beamed so brightly to wake all who were asleep.
It shone on the green field, **Sh**
And on the field was a farm, **FA**
On the farm was a farmhouse
And a little old barn **B over head**
And on the roof of the barn a rooster stood, **U u**
And crowed his morning song:
"Cock-a-doodle-doo, **k u u with jump**
Good morning to you, **u o u**
The day's begun, **D G**
There's work to be done **k d down**
Cock-a-doodle doo." (as above)

In the house, little Molly woke up, and she remembered it was a special day, but she
couldn't remember why. So she got out of bed, and shook her head, and began to be ready
for the day.

"This is the way I start my day (3x). This is the way I start my day, so early in the morning."
(skip to *Mulberry Bush* tune)

*So, she wa***sh***ed her face like this and she bru***sh***ed her teeth like that,*
*And she com***b***ed her hair that was clean and fair.*
Then she **p***ut on her dress, and her* **boo***ts*
And said her morning prayer: "In all I say, in all I do,
May strength and kindness shine right through."

When all this was done, she went into the kitchen, and there was mother with her apron on. And suddenly she remembered what day it was. Baking Day!

*"**B**aking day, (2x)*
*Oh, how I love **B**aking Day,*
*Yummy things to ea**t** we'll make,*
***S**weet delights, and **ch**ocolate cake.*
***B**aking Day (2x)*
How I love Baking Day."

*Molly: "**Goo**d m**o**rning, Mother."*
*Mother: "**Goo**d m**o**rning, Molly. Do you know what **d**ay it is?"*
*Molly: "Of course, I do. **(yes foot)** It's **B**aking Day."*
*Mother: "Yes. And wh**at** should we bake today?"*
*Molly: "I think I feel like, **m m m m**??? **Ch**ocolate **ch**ip cookies!"*
*Mother: "Very well, then. I have a**ll** the ingredients except for seven **e**ggs. Can you please go and fetch seven eggs from our hens outside."*

Molly was very happy to, and she picked up the basket and walked outside to where the hens lived.
"Now I'm going to (fetch the eggs) (3x)
Now I'm going to fetch the eggs
*For it's Baking Day." (Mulberry Bus**h** tune)*

*"**Sh**e put down her basket.*
*"**Goo**d m**o**rning dear hens."*
*"Clu**ck** (repeat)," said the hens.*
"Today is Baking Day and I need seven eggs please,
*And when all the **b**aking's **d**one,*
I'll bring a piece for everyone."
And then she gently put the eggs into the basket (count one to seven)
*"Thank y**o**u," said Molly. "Clu**ck** (repeat)," said the hens. And Molly went back to the kitchen. (skip or put feet down softly because of eggs)*

*Mother had all the ingredients out and they began to put them all into a big round bowl. They **p**oured in the flour and **b**utter and **s**ugar and **m**ilk and some **n**uts and **ch**ocolate **ch**ips and the **e**ggs, all seven. And with a big wooden spoon, Molly began to mix it all together:*
*"Mix to the left, and mix to the right, **m in all ways***
Mix up and down with all your might.
I can mix fast and I can mix slow,
But soon it will in the oven go."

When it was all mixed very well, they shaped the cookies to put on the baking tray.
"Round ones, flat ones, little ones and fat ones, small sounds to suit
All of different shapes and sizes,
When they're baked I'll eat the nicest."

Then they put them in the oven and had to wait for them to bake. Soon there was a delicious smell filling the kitchen. (**M m m m** by nose then tummy)
And finally Mother said:
"They are ready now, but they must first cool **d**own you see,
Then we'll have them for m**o**rning **t**ea."

And Molly remembered to take a piece for each hen.
"Here's a **p**iece for you...and a **p**iece for you...and a..."
"Cluck (5x) Thank **Y**ou."

Big Blue Boat
Based on a lesson by Jean Lynch

19
I love to sail in (my big blue boat) (3x) **B**
I love to sail in (my big blue boat) (2x)
My big blue boat it has (two white sails) (3x) etc. **U into L**
My big blue boat has (a flag on the top) (3x) etc. **F T**
We go for a row in my big blue boat, (we row and row) (2x) **R**
We go for a row in my big blue boat, (we row and row and row)
And all the fishes go (splish, splash, splish) (3x) etc. **f sh**
The wallowing whales they go spouting high **W T**
Deep underwater the seaweed swirls **D S**
The great big waves they go rolling by **W R or L**
My boat is rocking from side to side **Ei or D**
Brother wind he does give a big blow **W**
And there in front is a rock, and the boat is heading for the rock and...
My big blue boat, it has struck the rock (struck the great big rock) **K**
And now my boat it goes down and down **D**
And now we all have to swim and swim **M**
We come to the shore and we stand on the land **D with feet**
Drip goes the water, I'm wet, I'm wet **P wt**

First ending:
We run back home and we jump into bed **P** Good...bye...bye...bye.

Second ending:
How are we going to go home?
We'll have to build another boat.
First, we must saw the wood. **Zzz, zzz, zzz**, etc.
Now we must hammer the wood together. hammer (3x) knock (3x) (repeat, hammering fists together).
Now we must sew the sails (sit and sew round and round stitches for the sail and then up-and-down stitches for the flag)
What color shall we paint it? (yellow, rainbow...)
Now we're all going to paint our boat. **P**
And now we sail home in our new blue (yellow, rainbow...) boat. **B**

THE PETER STORIES ↝

These stories have been joyously done by the children, both in eurythmy and as pure dramatization or storytelling by the teacher. They can be added to and are suitable for ages three to six. Shy children cannot resist the "chewing" bits and can easily be enticed into joining in through that particular part. The following is as would be done for three-year-olds, e.g.: short sentences.

Once upon a time, there was a young boy called Peter. **T** *Peter woke up in the morning. A sunbeam came through the window and said:*
"Wake up, wake up, the sun shines bright, **e A e A**
The dark is conquered by the light." **D kk L** (later also with feet)
Peter jumped **P** *out of bed. He washed his face* **sh**. *He brushed his teeth* **r**. *He combed his hair* **m**. *He put on his clothes* **p**. *He ate his breakfast* **t to mouth**. *Mummy said, "Peter, go to the farmer and fetch a cabbage for supper* **B**, *I want to make cabbage soup."*
"All right, Mummy," said Peter, "I'll take my cart."

The wheels of the cart went round and round, the wheels of the cart went round and round **r** (*in circle*) *and he stopped* **T**. *There in front of him was a tortoise* **T head and t shoulders** (walk like a tortoise—get inside its skin!) *The tortoise stopped* **T** *and said, "Good morning, Peter.* **U O T** *Where are you going?"* **?** *"I'm going to the farm to get a big, big cabbage,"* **B** *said Peter.*

"May I come with you?" **E U** *asked the tortoise. "Yes,"* (foot position) *said Peter. The tortoise climbed into the cart and there he sat.* (**e** arms and legs crossed)

Peter pulled the cart and the wheels of the cart went round and round, the wheels of the cart went round and round, and he stopped. (as before)

There in front of him was a rabbit (put up hands to "bunny-ears" and hop). *"Hop, little bunny (3x) hop (3x) (repeat)." The rabbit stopped and said, "Good morning, Peter."* (repeat as for tortoise) *The rabbit climbed into the cart and there he sat next to the* **?** *tortoise!*

Peter pulled the cart, etc. There in front of him was a duck.

Put knees together, hands as tail and waddle—here one can quack with each waddle or add the following verse.

"Have you seen the little ducks going to the water (waddle)
Father, mother, baby duck, granny duck and grandpa,
Quack (7x)...quack (3x)...quack." (they love unexpected pauses here, **e small** with each quack, with hands and later feet)

Continue as above but drinking up the water **r up to mouth**, then swimming in the water **M**, then coming from the water. (waddle)

*The duck stopped and said, "Good morning Peter." (repeat as for others) And there he sat, next to the **?** tortoise, and next to the **?** rabbit!*

*And the wheels stopped. There in front of him was a frog **G** (jump like a frog). The frog said "Good morning (repeat as above)," into the cart hopped the frog, and sat next to the **?** tortoise, and the **?** rabbit, and the **?** duck!*

Peter pulled the cart, and the wheels...round. Peter came to the farm. Where was the farmer? He was chopping wood (clap hands and stamp feet from side to side)

Additional verse:

The axe swings, the steel rings
With a bang and a clang
And a leap it bites deep.

There are other verses but what is more important is repetition and rhythm.

The farmer stopped and said, "Good morning Peter, what do you want?"
"Good morning, Mr. Farmer," said Peter, "I want a cabbage, please."
"Pull one out yourself," said the farmer.

*Peter pulled and pulled and pulled **U** and up came the cabbage **B**, but when he wanted to put it in the cart. There sat the animals. He put the cabbage down, "Out," he said. **AU** The animals climbed out. Peter put the cabbage into the cart. **B** "What about me?" asked the tortoise, "What about me?" asked the rabbit, "What about me?" asked the duck, "What about me?" Asked the frog. **each time i with a finger** "You can sit on top!" **T** said Peter, and the animals climbed up, and Peter pulled the cart, and it was heavy! And the wheels of the cart went round...**R in circle**.*

All sit.

*Now, while Peter was pulling the cart, the tortoise said, "I'm hungry," **H out** The rabbit said, "I'm hungry," **H in** The duck said, "I'm hungry" **H out**. "Me too," said the frog. "Let's have just a nibble," they said.*

Animals eat; get "inside" each animal in turn.

The Tortoise went (chew with lips in, bite on them). *The rabbit went* (bottom lip tucked in and top teeth showing over). *The duck went* (both lips pouting well out). *The frog went* (tongue curling out and in beyond lips. Dwell on each type of chewing in sequence, then speed up. This part is so funny and the children cannot resist. It is also extremely healthy for them as it puts the will strongly into the mouth.

(whisper) *The cabbage was gone! And there they were, fast asleep, with full tummies!*

Snore: expansion and contraction with the arms. All stand.

And Peter pulled the cart, and the wheels of the cart went round...

Peter got home. There was his Mummy waiting for him. "Where is the cabbage, Peter??" she asked. "Behind me, Mummy," he said **B behind back**. *He looked behind and there were the animals, fast asleep. They looked so funny that Peter and his Mummy laughed and laughed. "Ha, ha, ha,"* etc. (Eurythmy therapy "laughter" is good here and the children love it—**shoulders H down into low A**.)

Peter's Mummy wasn't angry, but she said (pointer finger held up and moved from side to side in negation), *"Be careful, Peter, those animals can be naughty. But never mind. We'll have carrot soup for supper."*

The next time this story can be repeated with Peter going to fetch a **B**ig cauliflower, and his Mummy can warn him of the animals by using pointer finger as above. On the way back, they can just take a tiny nibble but again end up by finishing the whole cauliflower!

Also, Peter can take appropriate food for them and take them swimming. *"Where are you going Peter?" "I'm going swimming!"* **M**

A cabbage-leaf for the tortoise, a carrot for the rabbit and bread crumbs for the other two.

Here they do different types of swimming. In eurythmy, **L horizontal r** duck, **g** (one arm at a time) for frog and tortoise, the rabbit watches. They eat, and Peter has a sandwich (chew with mouth closed and upright to show the difference between human and animal). When he goes home, the duck and frog remain behind to swim some more.

Peter can also have a birthday party and invite the animals and then go into the making of the cake as well.

The children get to love the animals and their antics and, as a story on its own, many additions can be concocted. This story is a definite favorite because it is so funny, and children can relate to the animals.

Shoemaker—Blacksmith—Tailor ✤

There once was a Shoemaker, and he was so wee, **l little finger**
He lived in a hole in a very big tree **o T**
And he had a neighbor, and she was a mouse. **n m**
And she did his washing, and tidied his house. **Sh d**
Each morning at seven, he heard a wee tap, **tap pointer finger-tips together**
And in came the mouse, in her apron and cap. **m p**
She lit a wee fire, and fetched a wee broom, **f f u**
And she swept and she polished his little tree room. **s sh**
To take any wages she always refused. No, thank you,
So the cobbler said, "Thank you," and made her some shoes. **e u m**

"Tick-tack-too, tick-tack-too, **t t with fingers of one hand onto back of other alt.**
Tickety-tackety, tickety-tackety, tick-tack-too."

She put on her little pink shoes and off she went. (on tip-toe)
On her way she heard a little voice say, "What pretty shoes. Where did you get them?"
And there, in front of her, was a little **ff***airy.*
"From the cobbler, **b**
Who lives in a hole, in a very big tree." **o T**

Away flew the fairy.

12

Fly, fairy, fly, fly through the sky,
Flying here and flying there,
Flying, flying through the air,
Fly, fairy, fly, fly through the sky.
She came to the hole in the very big tree.
"Knock, knock, knock, Little door unlock." (clap rhythm) *and she waited* **e,**
"Knock, knock, knock, Little door unlock." (clap rhythm) *and she waited* **e,**
The door went open. There stood the cobbler.
"Cobbler, Cobbler, make my shoes, **b b m u** (use hands only)
Make them well by half-past two. **m a u**
Make them well that I may go, **m**
Dancing, dancing, to and fro." **d d skip**

Repeat "Tick-tack-too." (can be done with hands or feet repeated)
She thanked the shoemaker, put them on and tried them out.
"Point and point and point your toe,
Point them nicely, point them so. (in front)
Now we point from side to side, point them nicely, point them wide.

Now behind we point our toes, point them nicely, point them so.
Now we point across our feet, point them nicely, point them neat.
Now we roll them one by one, now together till we're done."
And away she flew. (Repeat "Fly, fairy, fly") And what did she hear below?
(make galloping sounds with feet .-.-.-)
It was a Prince galloping through the forest.

21

A Prince he went a-riding, a-riding, a-riding,
A Prince he went a-riding, on a bright summer's day.

And whoosh! **U** *Away went his horse's shoe. (limp to ._ rhythm)*
" My horse, is lame, my horse, is lame,
O woe, o woe, my horse, is lame." (repeat as necessary)

From which shoemaker do we get a horse-shoe? The Blacksmith!

There was the Blacksmith with all his children. They were very strong because they have
porridge for breakfast. (go around and feel their muscles)
First they make a big fire. **f f f f f f** *(flames from below upwards, repeat)*

"I am a Blacksmith, good and true, **B u**
Best of work I always do. **e D down**
Can you hammer one hammer like me?
Hammer, hammer, merrily. (hammer one fist on the open palm of the other hand and
change hands, later let the hammering-hand swing big)
"With rickety-tickety-tickety-tock." (2x)

This can be done in many ways. The best way is to keep fingers together to make a
strong hammer and slap the feet behind, right hand, right foot. This verse is repeated for two, three, four hammers and one can slap right hand, left foot crossed
behind. It is difficult, but they love it. Then use the right hand, left foot in front, etc.

Then the blacksmith put the horse's hoof between his legs from behind and knocked the
shoe on (rapid) rickety-tickety (many times). **k**
The Prince said, "Thank you," **e u***, and gave the blacksmith a* **B***ag of gold, and off he went.*
(Repeat: "The prince he went a-riding," etc., "galloping.")

The Prince and his horse were tired and so they went back to the castle. He put the horse in
the stable and gave all his horses some sugar.

Children stand nicely. Teacher goes to each one in turn with a bag of sugar, each child has to neigh and the teacher pops a lump of sugar into the open mouth—imaginary, of course!

Continuation:

The next morning, the Prince wondered if the Blacksmith could make him a new golden sword, so he rode back to the blacksmith.
"The prince he went a-trotting, a-riding, a-galloping (as before) on a bright summer's day."

"Please, Mr. Blacksmith, make me a sword, a golden sword **O***, a singing sword?* **S**
A calming sword, a taming sword **m***, a sword that brings you peace."* **S**
The blacksmith asked all his children to come and help, so they sat with their legs crossed.

Choose with the children what song to hammer onto the sword, e.g. *Rock-a-Bye-Baby, Twinkle, Twinkle Little Star*, etc. They take a golden hammer (two fingers of one hand) and beat the rhythm onto the palm of the other hand while singing. When they have "practiced" it they can beat it onto the sword. They love doing the following: The teacher conducts the "orchestra." Divide the circle into two halves. Whichever half the conductor points to beats the tune. After each phrase, put up your palm to stop them, then point to the other half, or single child, or whole lot to continue. When they can manage this, then chose someone to sit on your lap and help them to conduct. In this way they can make swords for the whole royal family!

The blacksmith gives the sword to the prince, who says, *"Thank you,"* and gives him a bag of gold. Then off he rides, swinging his sword. The children gallop around the circle swinging swords and singing. They love this.

The following is a good extension:

Then the prince wanted a new cloak to go with his beautiful sword, so he went to the tailor.
There was a little tailor sitting stitch, stitch, stitching, **t t t on backs of hands**
Cross-legged on the floor of his kitch, kitch, kitchen.
His **thumbs** *and his* **fingers** *they were nim, nim, nimble* **n n n**
With the needle and the cotton and the thim, thim, thimble. **i (finger) t m**
His fingers flew as swift as a swall, swall, swallow **f l**
And the needle and the cotton, it did foll, foll, follow. **l t l**

Then the horses can go to horse-training school (see page 102).

In this way the story can extend over six weeks, if not much longer. Parts can be repeated, cut out, added, etc.

The Prince can also go to the dwarfs for gold for a crown, then back to the blacksmith. The theme is endless.

GOLDILOCKS

Once upon a time, there was a little girl called Goldilocks. **O**
A sunbeam came and tickled her on the cheek and said:
"Wake up (2x), the sun shines bright, **e a e a A**
The dark is conquered by the light." **d kk l**

She jumped out of bed **p**. *She washed her face* **sh**. *She brushed her teeth* **r**. *She put on her*
clothes **P** *and said "Mummy, is breakfast ready?" "No," said her Mummy.*
Goldilocks went for a walk.
"Now I'm walking (in the woods) (3x) (Mulberry Bush tune)
Now I'm walking in the woods
For it's a lovely day."
(skipping, hopping, stamping, tip-toe)

She came to a little house. She knocked on the door:
"Knock (3x) Little door unlock." (pause)

Repeat, but every time louder, starting with clapping on every syllable, end with
clapping and stamping on each with the children even screaming the words, give a
slight pause, then capture them again by repeating very softly. The children love this,
and it can be used for all sorts of stories.

She opened the door and went inside.
There on the table were three bowls of porridge: There was a great big bowl, there was a
middle-sized bowl, and there was a teeny-weeny baby bowl. **B b b three sizes**

Goldilocks was hungry.
She tasted a little porridge from the great big bowl, but it was too hot! **t h**
She tasted the porridge from the middle-sized bowl, but it was too cold! **t k**
She tasted the porridge from the teeny-weeny baby bowl and it was just right,
so she ate and she ate and she ate until it was all gone. **t t t g**

Then she saw three chairs. There was a great big chair. There was a middle-sized chair, and
there was a teeny-weeny baby chair. **B b b three sizes**
She sat down on the great big chair, and it was too hard. **S H**
She sat down on the middle-sized chair, and it was too soft. **s s**

She sat down on the baby chair and it was just right, so there she sat **s e** *and it went crack,*
crack, crack and she fell doomps! on the floor. **K k k d**

Goldilocks went upstairs. (play or sing the scale going up, hands go as steps from low
to high)
In the bedroom there were three beds.
There was a great big bed, there was a middle-sized bed, and there was teeny-weeny baby
bed. (2x **B** as before)

She lay down on the great big bed, but it was too hard.
She lay down on the middle-sized bed, but it was too soft.
She lay down on the teeny-weeny baby bed, and it was just right, so there she lay. And she fell fast asleep. **L**

Who lived in that house? The three bears!
Heavy, heavy Daddy bear walks, heavily over the ground.
Softly, softly Mummy bear walks, she doesn't make a sound,
Quickly, quickly baby bear walks, he skips round and round and round and round.
Repeat using only the sound **B** from loud and stamping to soft and small skips.

Another bear verse could be:
"I'm a big, brown, bristly, bushy bear,
I rumble and tumble through bush and through bramble,
I'm a big, brown, bristly, bushy bear.
I'm a mommy brown, etc.
I'm a baby brown," etc. **B b b three sizes walking**

The door was open **P***, someone had been there.*
They went inside. "Who's been eating my porridge?" (deep voice) **U RR**
(repeat with medium voice)
(repeat with small voice) *"And look, it's all gone, boo-hoo."* **G then B over head**

"Who's been sitting on my chair?" **U S CH**
(repeat) *"And look, it's all broken, broken, broken. Boo-hoo!* **K B**

They went upstairs. First went Daddy Bear (scale going up as Goldilocks)
"Who's been sleeping on my bed?"
(same with Mummy and baby bear) *"And look, there she is!"* **U e**

Stand in **e** arms and legs while the following is said:
Now when Goldilocks heard (deep voice), *"Who's been sleeping in my bed?" she knew she was fast asleep. When she heard* (soft voice), *"Who's been sleeping in my bed?" then she knew she was dreaming. When she heard* (high voice) *"Who's been sleeping in my bed?" then she KNEW she was awake. She saw the three bears standing there, and she got such a fright that she jumped out of bed.* **P jump with arms legs** *She jumped* **P** *to the window. She jumped out of the window. She jumped to the ground. She jumped over the daisy bush, she jumped over the rose bush, she jumped over the gate, and she skipped all the way home.* (the children love the repeat P)

This is a wholesome healthy story because it has so many elements of repetition, contraction and expansion, loud/soft and **B**'s.

THE PANCAKE STORY

Once upon a time there was a mother who made pancakes for her children. This made her children very happy and they danced and sang:

22

"Fire, fire burning, pancake is turning, **f f e e palms up, t turn once**
Eggs and flour, milk so sweet **e 2 fingers, l**
Pancakes today we'll eat." **e e d t to mouth**

But the mother had to go out, and she asked the children to look after the pancake for her. This they did, but when they looked out of the window and saw: **U** *the sun shining in the garden* **A***, the flowers growing* **L***, the worms creeping* **r***, the beetles grabbeling* **b***, the butterflies flying* **l***, or the snow falling, the leaves falling (depending on the season).*

They said:

23

"See the lovely shining sun, **A**
In the garden we will run
Let us walk (skip) out of the gate **G**
Our pancake it can wait."

The poor pancake got very hot in the pan and cried out:
"Fire, fire burning, pancake is turning **f f e e t** *(can turn once)*
If you burn me black as coal **e fists**
Out I'll jump and away I'll roll." **P r**

24

"I jumped out of the pan and away I ran, **P r**
I roll like a ball, and I know I won't fall."

The pancake rolled on and on and he met two rabbits (rabbits hop)
"We are the rabbits and we can hop
Oh please, dear pancake, won't you stop, **i e e T**
A tiny bite we'd like to try **t to mouth**
Oh, pancake, please don't pass us by." **e e i**

"No, No," said the pancake. **n n**
"I jumped out of the pan and away I ran
From the rabbits who hop (hop)
I roll like a ball, and I know I won't fall."

The pancake rolled on and on and he met two cats, (walk like cats)

"We are the cats **k t** *to shoulder and we chase rats,* **rr t**
Oh, please, dear pancake, won't you stop
A tiny bite we'd like to try
Oh, pancake, please don't pass us by."

"No, No," said the pancake,
"I jumped out of the pan...who hop
And the cats who catch rats...won't fall."

The pancake rolled on and on, and he met two pigs, **g**
"We are two pigs and we dance jigs (dance)
Oh, please, dear pancake, won't you stop,
A tiny bite...pass us by."

"No, No" said the pancake,
"I jumped out of the pan...catch rats,
And the pigs who dance jigs...won't fall."

The pancake rolled on and on and met two mice. (tip-toe like mice)
"We are the mice, so sweet and nice, **m**
Oh, please, dear pancake, etc....pass us by."
"No, No." said the pancake,
"I jumped out of the pan...sweet and nice."

The pancake rolled on and on, and he met the children.
The children asked, " Please dear pancake, may we eat you?" **i t to mouth**

And the pancake said, "Yes, you may. I did not want to be gobbled **b b up**, *but I do want to*
be eaten by you, **t** *if you have good manners and say grace."*

(fold hands) *"Thank you, dear pancake, you are yummy,*
You taste so good right to my tummy,
And for making him?
We thank Mummy!"

The Little Red Hen

There was once a Little Red Hen who lived on a farm together with a duck, **d down and knees together** *a cat* **k t to shoulders** *and a dog* **d down and lean over**.
One day, the Little Red Hen was scratching and scratching and scratching in the farm yard **r with feet** *when she found some grains of wheat.*
"Who will help me plant the wheat?" she said. **U e a**
"Not I," said the duck, "Quack" (3x). **n e e e**
"Not I," said the cat, "Prrrr (3x)". **n kt rrr**
"Not I," said the dog, "Woofff (3x)". **n d wuff**
"Then I will do it myself!" she said. **e d e**

"Scratch and scratch and scratch the ground, **r**
Scratch it with my feet,
Dig and dig and dig the ground, **g**
I'm going to plant the wheat."

And she scratched **r** *the ground and she dug* **g** *the ground and in went the grains of wheat.*
She covered it with earth, and she said her magic verse. **v**
"Father Sun, shine on my wheat and make it grow. **A O**
Sister Rain, rain on my wheat and make it grow. **R O**
Brother Wind, blow on my wheat and make it grow." **W O**
And it did grow. It grew and it grew and it grew and it became golden. **U O**

"Who will help me cut the wheat?" asked the Little Red Hen **u k**
"Not I," said the duck, "Quack (3x)."
"Not I," said the cat, "Prrrr (3x)."
"Not I," said the dog, "Woofff (3x)."
"Then I will do it myself!" she said. **e d e**

"Cut and cut and cut the wheat, cut the wheat right down, **k**
Cut and cut and cut the wheat, cut it to the ground."

"Who will help me thresh the wheat?" asked the Little Red Hen. **u sh**
"Not I," said the duck, "Quack (3x)."
"Not I," said the cat, "Prrrr (3x)."
"Not I," said the dog, "Woofff (3x)."
"Then I will do it myself!" she said.

And she thresshhed and thresshhed and thresshhed the wheat. (repeat) **sh**

When she had threshed the wheat, she said,
"Who will help me take the wheat to the Miller to grind it into flour?" **U R**

"Not I," said the duck, "Quack (3x)."
"Not I," said the cat, "Prrrr (3x)." "Not I," said the dog, "Woofff (3x)."
"Then I will do it myself!" she said.

And she put the wheat into a wheelbarrow and pushed it to the Miller **U in front**
And the wheels of the wheelbarrow went round and round (repeat)

This can be repeated while the teacher leads them in a "snake" all around the room doing **R** low down as a wheel, then back into a circle.

Then the Miller ground and ground it into flour. (2x) **R**

When it was all ground into flour, the Little Red Hen said,
"Who will help me bake some bread?" **B**
"Not I," said the duck, "Quack (3x)."
"Not I," said the cat, "Prrrr (3x)."
"Not I," said the dog, "Woofff (3x)."
"Then I will do it myself!" she said.

She put in the flour **L***, and milk* **l***, and eggs* **e***,* (and anything else the children can think of, i.e. nuts, raisins). *And she mixed it all together.* **M** (the children can do this endlessly with no audible sound) *She put it into the oven* **O** *and she waited.* (sniff deliciously)

When the bread was ready, the Little Red Hen said,
"Who is going to help me eat the bread?" **U t**
"Me!" said the duck. **i with finger**
"Me!" said the cat.
"Me!" said the dog.
"Oh, no, you won't," said the Little Red Hen. **neg**
"I will eat it myself!" **t e**
And she called all her little chickens and they ate it all up. **L t t**

The Little Red Hen And The Fox ❀

This story can be used as a sequel to the other Little Red Hen story. If it is used as such then one must create a link, e.g. *the little red hen and the cat decided to go and live in a little hut in a forest. Also in the hut was a little mouse.*

Once upon a time, there lived somewhere in the forest in a little hut a cat, a mouse, and a little red hen. The cat had a soft little basket, prrr, prrr, the mouse had a deep little hole, squee, squee, and the little red hen had a high pole on which she could roost.

One morning the little red hen said, "Who will help me make a fire in the oven?" "Not I," said the cat, "Prrr (3x)." "Not I," said the mouse, "Squee (3x)." "Then I will do it myself," she said. And so she did.

"Fire, fire, flickering fire,
Flaming (3x) higher." (repeat if necessary)

When the fire was burning, the little red hen said, "Who will help me sweep the room?" "Not I," said the cat, "Prrr (3x)." "Not I." said the mouse. "Squee (3x)." "Then e *I will do* d *it myself," she said. And so she did. "Here I go (a-sweeping). (2x)*
Here I go (a-sweeping) (2x) up the room. W

When the room was swept, the little red hen said, "Who will help me cook the breakfast?" "Not I," said the cat, "Prrr (3x)." "Not I," said the mouse, "Squee (3x)." "Then I will do it myself," she said. And so she did.
"Pancakes (3x) for breakfast,
Pancakes (2x) with honey on the top."

When she had cooked the breakfast, the little red hen said, "Who will help me eat the breakfast?" "Me!" said the cat, "Prrr (3x)." "Me!" said the mouse, "Squee (3x)."
"No, I am going to eat it all up myself," said the little red hen, "unless you both promise me that you will always help me!"
"I will," said the cat, "I will," said the mouse.
And so the little red hen shared the breakfast with them.

When they had eaten, the little red hen looked out of the window, and who did she see on the road? The fox!
"The fox is coming!" she cried and flew U *to the top of her roost.*
"The fox is coming!" cried the cat and curled up in the basket.
"The fox is coming!" (small f m) *squeaked the mouse and crept into his little hole.*

The fox stepped into the room.
"Good morning, little mouse! Good morning, cat! Good morning, little red hen! Which one of you will scratch my back?"
"Not I," n *said the cat. "Not I." said the mouse* n. *"Then I will," said the little red hen.*

And she scratched and scratched the fox's back. She scratched it all the way **up** to his ears and she scratched it all the way down to his tail and when she scratched it up to his ears again he lifted his paw and struck her to the floor and bundled her into his big bag. **B**

"Now who will help me?" cried the little red hen from the bag.
"Not I," **n** said the cat **k t** and ducked into her basket. "Not I," **n** said the mouse **m**, and ducked into his hole **o**. The fox grabbed **b** the cat from her basket and bundled her into the bag. **B's** And he grabbed the mouse from its hole and bundled it into the bag with the little red hen. He put the bag over his shoulder and went home. **B over back, walk**.
It was a hot day, and after a while the big bag with the cat, the mouse and the little red hen inside became too heavy for the fox. He put it down onto the ground **D**, lay down in the shade of a tree and fell asleep **L**. The little red hen then took a little pair of scissors from under her wing and a needle and cotton and said, "Who **u** will cut **k** with the scissors?" **s**
"Me," said the cat **i finger**
"And m**e**," said the mouse. So, strongly together they cut **k** open the sack and jumped out. **p**

Once they were out, the little red hen said, "Who will fetch some stones?" "Me," said the cat.
"And me," said the mouse. So, strongly **together** they brought three stones and placed them in the bag.

When the stones were in the bag **B**, the little red hen said, "Who will sew **s** up the sack?"
"Me," said the cat, "And me," said the mouse. So, strongly **together** they sewed up the bag and ran home. Ever since then the cat and the mouse have **always** helped the little red hen.

And what did the fox do? He woke up **K** grabbed the bag **B**, put it over his shoulder and went home, but the bag felt much heavier (heavy steps). When he came near his house he called, "Mother, put the big glass pot on the stove **O**. I am bringing supper."

Above the pot with the water, which was now boiling, was the chimney. So the fox thought that the best way to get the animals into the pot was to throw them down the chimney.

The fox climbed up the roof **B B B** and threw the bag down the chimney. **D down** The stones fell down sssmashhh into the glass dish and it all went crrrasshhh over the floor.

Never again **negation** did the fox try to catch the little red hen, for he knew that she was far too clever for him.

The Golden Ball ☙

Mary (any name) had (a golden ball) (3x) **O**
Mary had a golden ball, she threw it in the air. **O U**
It rolled and rolled (upon the ground) (2x) **R**
It rolled and rolled upon the ground
And fell into a hole. **O**

She looked into the hole, **U down**
A slithery snake came (sliding out) (3x) **S**
A slithery snake came sliding out
Out of the hole in the ground
"My golden ball, my golden ball, **O**
Please give me my golden ball." **I arm only down, O**
The slithery snake went sliding down, **S**
Down in the hole in the ground.

Mary looked into the hole. Out hopped a rabbit (hands up for ears)
"My golden ball, my golden ball, (same as above)
Please give me my golden ball."
"Can't," **N** *said the rabbit, "I saw the farmer with his rake,* **r r** (can do sounds with ears)
So I go quickly the carrots to take."
And off he hopped (music or rabbit-hopping song).

Mary looked into the hole. Out slithered a snail (two fingers each side of forehead and
  slide feet)
"My golden ball,..."
"Can't," said the snail, **n** (speak slowly for snail)
"I have a big house upon my back, **B behind back**
If I bend down it will surely crack."
And off he went (slow music or snail verse—drag feet slowly and make horns with
  fingers).

Mary looked into the hole. Out came a butterfly **L**
"My golden ball..."
"Can't," said the butterfly,
"My wings, they are so soft and small, **S**
I cannot carry up the ball." **L** *and away she flew* (fly **L** with verse or music).

Other animals can also come out when repeating the story.

Mary, she (began to cry) (3x) **ei**
Mary, she began to cry, "My golden ball is gone!" **O G**

"I'll get it for you," said a little voice.
Mary looked into the hole, and there she saw a little dwarf. **U dff**
"First I must finish my hammering," and he took his little hammer.
The following is loved by the children, and don't be afraid to scream with them as it
is very easy to quieten them again. One fist hammers on the other with each word.
As they get louder, feet can stamp in time as well. They also join in the words.

"Hammer (3x), knock (3x)." (pause) Repeat, getting louder each time until all scream.
Then softly hammer one "pointer" finger on the other.
"Now the golden hammer—hammer (3x), knock (3x),
And now the silver hammer—(little fingers). *Hammer (3x), knock (3x)*
Silver, shining, golden, bright,
Brighter than the moon at night."

Then he took the ball (crouch down) *and called out, "Mary, are you ready? And she called*
"Ye-es" and whooops! **U** *Up came the ball, and Mary caught it, and she said, "Thank you,*
Dwarfie." **E U Dff** *and she skipped all the way home.*

The Golden Goose

Wording based on a play by Catherine and Peter V. Alphen. Contraction and expansion verse by
Molly von Heide.

There was once a man who had three sons, the youngest of whom was called Dummeling.
DL
His brothers teased him, "You are stupid, you are silly, **U S U S**
You are just a silly billy!" **U S**
And they laughed at him, "Ha! Ha! Ha! (3x) Ho! (3x)" **laugh with H shoulders**

That night:
The horses went into the stable and
The cows went into the barn, and
The dogs went into the kennels, and (whole circle contracts)
The cats went into baskets, and
The mice went into the hole, and
Everybody slept, except for the owl which went twit-twoo.

In the morning:
The mice came out of the hole, and
The cats came out of the baskets, and
The dogs came out of the kennels, and (circle expands)
The cows came out of the barn, and (arms expand)
The horses came out of the stables, and the sun came up.

The following verse is optional.

"Wake up, wake up, the sun shines bright, **e A, e A,**
The dark is conquered by the light." **D k k L**

The oldest brother said, "I'm going to the forest, to cut some wood." **G F K D**
His mother gave him a bottle of sweet wine and piece of cake. **b e**

"Now I'm going to the wood, to the wood, to the wood,
Now I'm going to the wood, with my cake and wine (tune of *London Bridge*).
It's a lovely, (lovely day) (3x) and I feel just fine."

He stopped. **T** *There in front of him was an old man, who said to him:*
"Please, give me some of your cake, **l arm, e palms up**
And a sip of your wine I will gladly take." **p to mouth, e**

"Oh No! If I give you my cake and my lovely wine too **neg**
There'll be none for myself, so be off with you!" **N F**
(or)
"Not at all, not a bit **N b**
Not a crumb, not a sip! **r p**
Be off with you!" **F**

Stamp feet from side to side and clap hands in time to the verse.

The axe swings, the steel rings,
With a thud from below,
A sharp edge cuts a wedge,
The axe swings, the steel rings
With a bang and a clang,
And a leap it bites deep. (repeat if necessary, short, short, long rhythm)

The axe flew up into the air, went round and round and cut! **U r r k on arm**
"My arm is sore, my arm is sore, **A O A O**
O woe! O woe! My arm is sore." **O up, O down, A O**
(or; *"Boo hoo (2x) My arm is sore."*) **B over head**

He got home (walk slowly) *and his mother put a bandage around it and put him to bed.* **b B**

That night:
The horses went into the stable, etc. Story continues as above as for the first brother
but second brother cuts his leg and limps home. (short long rhythm) *...and put him*
to bed.

Repeat: *That night, etc.*

Then Dummeling said, "I am going to the forest to cut some wood."
His brothers laughed at him, "Ha! (3x) Ho! (3x), **shoulders h-a h-o**
You are stupid, don't you know! **S**
We have cut our arm and leg, **k A e**
You will surely cut your head!" **U k H up from head**

His mother gave to him some sour bread that had been baked in the ashes, and some sour beer. **b Sh b** *but Dummeling didn't mind.*

"Now I'm going (to the wood) (3x)
Now I'm going to the wood, with sour bread and beer!"
He stopped. There, in front of him was the old man who said to him, "Please, give me some of your cake, and a sip of your wine I will gladly take."

"I've only ash-bread and sour beer too, **sh b**
It's not very nice, but I'll share it with you." **n sh u**
They sat down to eat. And when Dummeling took out his bread and beer, he found that it had turned into cake and wine. So they ate and ate and ate. **t to mouth** *And when they had finished eating the old man said, "You have a good heart—see that tree with the shoots?* **A T** *Cut it down, and look at the roots."* **k d u**

The axe swings... etc. Stop.
"What's there at the roots that I can see? **U**
A Golden Goose just for me, me, me! **G i i i alt. hands**
Look, oh, look, and see (3x) **U jump i jump hands and feet**
A golden goose just for me (3x)." (can be repeated joyously) **G also press knees to-gether**
He picked up the goose, put it under his arm and off he went.

25

"Walk along, walk along, walk along with me,
I have found a golden goose, under the roots of a tree.
Skip along, (hop, trot, dance, tip-toe, gallop, etc.)"
Soon Dummeling came to a town. He went to an inn to stay the night. The innkeeper had three daughters. They were greedy, and when they saw the golden feathers they wanted one. **greed soul gesture** *Dummeling went up the stairs to his room, put the goose down on the table and went out.*

The oldest daughter tip-toed up the stairs to the room (soft tip-toe steps going up a scale). She put out her hand and touched a feather and she stuck! **K**
"I'm stuck! I'm stuck! Oh woe, oh woe! **Stay in K**
The golden goose won't let me go!"

The second daughter tip-toed (same). She touched her sister and she stuck!
"...won't let us go!"

The third daughter...etc.

Dummeling came into the room. He put the golden goose under his arm and off he went with the three sisters stuck behind, like this.

In the circle let each child place one hand on the shoulder of the one in front, preferably alternate hands, with one hand/arm free to contract and expand **H**. The teacher leads the "stuck" children in all directions.

26
"Help, help, I can't get loose,
For I must follow the golden goose,
Help, help, I can't get free,
Won't somebody please help me!"

They passed a priest who called out, "Come away girls, for shame!" **M** *and he tried to pull them away, and he stuck!* (continue song) **K**
They passed the servant of the priest who tried to pull the priest away, and he stuck! **K** (continue song)
He passed some farmers who pulled at them, and they stuck! (continue song, etc., then stop).

Now the King had a daughter who was always sad and never laughed. **sadness**
The King said that whoever made her laugh could marry her.
"Oh, the day is dull and dreary, **O up, D down**
Oh, the world is sad and weary **O up, S down**
With a tear and with a sigh **T to eyes, E l**
We must live until we die." **L D down**
And she looked out of her window and saw...(quickly go back into "stuck" line)
"Help, help, I can't get loose, for I must follow the golden goose..."

"But look who comes, Oh ha, ha, hee, **U H**
What a funny sight to see
Ha, ha, ha, Oh, deary me, **H shoulders**

Ha, ha, ho, ho, hee, hee, hee!" **into A, then O then I**
But would the King let Dummeling marry the princess?
"No! Bring me first a man who can drink his fill, **neg. R to mouth**
A cellar full of wine, not a drop to spill." **L**

At this point one can enact with the children how the farmers picked the grapes, put them in a big vat, washed their feet, trod the grapes, put them through a sieve into barrels, with sugar, and do big **B**'s for, *"Here is a barrel, and here is a barrel,* etc.

"The little old man was kind and good
I will seek him in the wood."

But when he came into the forest he saw a man who was sorrowful.

"Alas, alack, Oh misery, **S down**
Who knows the thirst that's torturing me? **U**
Water's tasteless, cold and wet, **negation**
A barrel of wine I've drunk and yet **B**
I'm thirsty, thirsty as can be **S**
If only I could drink the sea!" **R up**

Dummeling said, "Now come, I know a cellar fine, **M in**
Full to the brim, with barrels of wine. **B**
Where you may satisfy your thirst **S**
Where you may drink until you burst!" **R**

Dummeling took him to the cellar, and there was a barrel and he drank, and drank and drank. And there was another barrel and he drank, and drank, and drank (repeat as much as necessary). **B R**

*Dummeling went to the King. "Pl**ea**se may I **m**arry the **p**rincess?"* **i m P**

"No! Bring me a man who can eat and eat **N T to mouth**
A mountain of bread and think it a treat." **T B**

At this point one can extend, if wanted, into making a mountain of bread—huge basin, flour and more flour, and many eggs, etc and asking the sun to shine extra hot to bake it and it rises higher and higher, etc.

Dummeling went into the forest and there he saw a man who was pulling his belt tighter and tighter. **B**

"Alas, alack, Oh misery. Who knows the hunger biting me? **S U H in**
I've munched an oven-load of bread. **B**
Without some more I'll soon be dead! **D**
I'm hungry, hungry as can be **H out and in**
Please help a starving man like me!" **l arm**

"The King has promised, so he said,
To bake a mountain out of bread **T B**
So come with me and eat your fill **M**
If you can eat through such a hill." **T L**

The man ate and ate, and ate, etc. **T alt. arms to mouth**

Dummeling went to the King. "Please may I marry the princess?"

"No! Bring me a boat, if you want my daughter, **B**
That can sail on the land and on water." **L**

Dummeling went to the forest. There he met the old man who said to him,
"You've been good and kind to me **u**
Look over there, and you will see **U**
A ship that stands upon the shore, **P sh**
The strangest ship you ever saw **P**
That swiftly sails on land and sea, **L**
My gift to you, who gave to me." **U m in**
Dummeling thanked the old man and got into the boat.

19
All go round in the circle. **L**
"I love to sail in my beautiful boat,
It sails on the land, it sails on the sea.
I love to sail in my beautiful boat
That sails on the land and the sea."

Dance.

The wedding bells rang far and wide
Dummeling has won his bride,
He'll be our King in time to come
And now, at last, our tale is done.

THE HUNGRY CAT
Based on a Norwegian Tale

A hungry cat is on his way. Prrrr, prrrr, prrrr, prrrr (walk as cat **R** arms and legs, let
children join in saying rrrrrrr because it makes the tongue mobile)
He looks for food, he looks for prey. **U U**
"Now tell me true, and who are you?" **U A U**

"I'm the man with the axe, the woodcutter good, (clap rhythm and stamp)
A-cutting the trees and chopping the wood. **K T** (then clap and stamp)
Good day, Mr. Cat, and how are you? (slowly) **U D k t** (shoulders) **Au in, A U**
You've come a long way. Did you eat well today?" **G T to mouth**

"Oh, no! Just half an egg and a little stew. **N a e hands, s**
*And I'm **h**ungry still, so I'll go**bb**le up you!"*
*And he go**bb**led up the wood-cutter, too.*
*(or: "But now I'll eat y**ou** and I'll have my fill, for I am **h**ungry, **h**ungry still.)*

A hungry cat is on his way. Prrrr, prrrr, prrrr, prrrr,
He looks for food and he looks for prey.
"Now tell me true, and who are you?"

"I'm the little girl with the pretty curl, **L** (as curls and skip from side to side)
A-dancing along and singing a song.
Good day Mr. Cat, and how are you?
You've come a long way, did you eat well today?"

"Oh, no! Just half an egg and a little stew,
And the man with the axe, the wood-cutter good, (clap and stamp)
A-cutting the trees and chopping the wood. As above
But I'm hungry still and I'll gobble up you!"
And he gobbled up the little girl, too.

A hungry cat is on his way, Prrrr, prrrr, prrrr, prrrr,
He looks for food and he looks for prey.
"Now tell me true, and who are you?"
I'm the little gnome who lives under a stone. **O over head** (crouch down then rise)
Good day, Mr Cat, and how are you?
You've come a long way, did you eat well today?"

"Oh, no! Just half an egg and a little stew,
And the man with the axe, the wood-cutter good
A-cutting the trees and chopping the wood;
And the little girl with the pretty curl,

A-dancing along and singing a song.
But I'm hungry still and I'll gobble up you!"
And he gobbled up the little gnome, too!

A hungry cat is on his way, Prrr, prrr, prrr, prrr,
He looks for food and he looks for prey.
"Now tell me true, and who are you?"

"I am the snail called Oh-so-slow. (walk slowly sliding feet—fingers as horns)
I carry my house wherever I go.
Good day, Mr. Cat, and how are you? (slowly)
You've come a long way, did you eat well today?"

"Oh, no! Just half an egg and a little stew,
And the man with the axe, the woodcutter good,
A-cutting the trees and chopping the wood;
And the little girl, with the pretty curl,
A-dancing along and singing a song;
And the little gnome who lives under a stone
But I'm hungry still, and I'll gobble up you!"
And he gobbled up the little snail, too!

A hungry cat is on his way, Prrr, prrr, prrr, prrr,
He looks for food and he looks for prey.
"Now tell me true, and who are you?"
I am the goat called Capricorn, **P**
With the shaggy coat and the golden horn. **Sh g o gh** (in by head as horns)
Good day, Mr. Cat, and how are you?
You've come a long way. Did you eat well today?"

"Oh, no! Just half an egg and a little stew,
And the man with the axe, the wood-cutter good,
A-cutting the trees and chopping the wood;
And the little girl, with the pretty curl,
A-dancing along and singing a song;
And the little gnome who lives under a stone;
And the little snail called Oh-so-slow,
Who carries his house wherever he may go.
But I'm hungry still and I'll gobble up you!"

"No! oh, you greedy cat, that will never do. **Big N N**
With my golden horns I will finish you." **g o h**
(expand the circle, all put heads down, make horns, contract circle to center)
BIFF! **"explode" B** (the children will want to do this repeatedly)
Out came the snail called Oh-so-slow,
Who carries his house wherever he may go.
Out came the little gnome who lived under the stone,
Out came the little girl with the little curl, a-dancing along and singing a song.
Out came the man with the axe, the wood-cutter good
A-cutting the trees and chopping the wood.

And they all said, "Thank you goat called Capricorn, **E U P**
With the shaggy coat and the golden horn. Thank You!" **Sh go H E U**

The Louse and The flea ✐

A louse and a flea kept house together and were **b**usy **b**rewing **b**eer in an **e**ggshell.
The **l**ittle **l**ouse fell in and **b**urnt herself. At this the little **f**lea began to scream and scream
and scream. (all sounds with fingers and hands with "scream." The **l** can be done with
pointed toes as well)

In the room there was a door and the little door said, "Little flea, why are you screaming?"
D F ?
"Because the little louse has burnt herself." **L pointers**
"Then," said the little door, "I will creak, and creak and creak." **R with shoulders only**

In the corner was a little broom and the little broom said, "Little door, why are you creak-
ing and creaking?" **U D R shoulders**
"Have I not reason to creak? **R**
The little flea is weeping and weeping **W W**
Because the little louse has burnt herself."
"Then," said the little broom, "I will sweep and sweep and sweep." (continue with **S**)

Then a little cart was passing by (**R** while going round in the circle) *and the little cart*
stopped and said, "Little broom, why are you sweeping and sweeping?" **U S**
"Have I not reason to sweep?" said the little broom,
Because the little door is creaking and creaking,
Because the little flea is screaming and screaming,
Because the little louse has burnt herself."
"Then," said the little cart, "I will run," and it began to run, and run, and run. **R**

It stopped because there in front of it was a little ash-heap. **P**
And the ash-heap said, "Little cart, why are you running and running?" **R**
"Have I not reason to run?" said the little cart,
Because the little broom is sweeping and sweeping,
Because the little door is creaking and creaking,
Because the little flea is screaming and screaming,
Because the little louse has burnt herself."
"Then," said the ash-heap, "I will begin to flicker and flame and flare." **f-f-f** (from low
up as a fire)

A little tree stood near the ash-heap, and the little tree said, "Ash-heap, why are you flam-
ing?" **T P F**
"Have I not reason to flame?" said the ash-heap,
Because the little cart is running and running,
Because the little broom is sweeping and sweeping,
Because the little door is creaking and creaking,
Because the little flea is screaming and screaming,
Because the little louse has burnt herself."
"Then," said the little tree, "I will shake myself," and she shook, and shook and shook herself
so that her leaves fell down, down, down. **Sh sh d d d**

A little girl was skipping to the river and she was carrying a water-pitcher. (skip around in
the ring)
And the little girl stopped and said, "Little **t**ree, why do you **sh**ake yourself?"
"Have I not reason to shake myself?" said the little tree,
Because the ash-heap is flaming and flaming,
Because the little cart is running and running,
Because the little broom is sweeping and sweeping,
Because the little door is creaking and creaking,
Because the little flea is screaming and screaming,
Because the little louse has burnt herself."

"Then," said the little girl, "I will break my water-pitcher." And she broke her water-pitcher.
Bk Bk

Nearby flowed a river, and the water in the river said, "Little girl, why do you break your
water-pitcher?" **V Bk**
"Have I not reason to break my water-pitcher?" said the little girl,
Because the little tree is shaking and shaking,
Because the little ash-heap is flaming and flaming,
Because the little cart is running and running,
Because the little broom is sweeping and sweeping,
Because the little door is creaking and creaking,

Because the little flea is screaming and screaming,
Because the little louse has burnt herself."
"Then," said the water, "I will begin to flow." And it began to flow, and the water flowed over the little water-pitcher, and it flowed over the little girl, and it flowed over the little tree, and it flowed over the ash-heap, and it flowed over the little cart, and it flowed over the little broom, and it flowed over the little door, and it flowed over the little flea, and it flowed over the little louse, and it flowed on and on and on.

Do **w** or **v up and down slowly** and dreamily around in the circle. Whenever it flows over something one can do a turn then flow gently onwards. All the children do everything.

As a change when the children know the lesson, they can be divided into the various characters, and the teacher then does all the parts from one to the other. For the cart, four children can hold hands making a square, all facing forward so that they can run.

THE THREE GNOMES ✿

There were once three little gnomes. They were very good friends. They were called Noddily-krinklecroot, **n k u** Noddily-krinklemight, **n k t shoulders** and Short-short-long **clap rhythm**. Such strange names!

The wind blew through the trees, "Shzzz, shzzz, shzzz. Who are you?" **U A U**
"Me? I'm Noddily-krinklecroot, **i finger, n k u**
I sit and squat beneath the root, **S down into squatting, u**
Who brings the shoot up to the light? **U from down up into upright**
Me! Me! Me! With Noddily-krinklemight!" **i i i n k t**

The rain rained through the air, "Who are you?" **R U A U**
"Me? I'm Noddily... " (repeat)

The sun shone in the heavens, "Who are you?" **A**
"Me? I'm Noddily..." (repeat)

He picked up his little bag and went to visit his friend. **b**

"Little dwarfs so short and strong,
Heavy footed march along,
Every head is straight and proud
Every step is firm and loud." (or any other dwarf marching song)

He came to the house of his friend Noddily-krinklemight who lived under the roots of a big tree. He knocked at the door, "Knock (3x), little door unlock!" (clap to rhythm), and he waited. **e** *He knocked again, "Knock (3x), little door unlock!" And he waited.*

The little gnome crept from his home, **O above head from squatting to upright**
"M'thinks I feel a raindrop near **i finger**
Drip, drop, drip, drop, drizzle on the tree-top, **d (5x) T t**
Rain (4x), I go back in my home again!" **R O down to squatting again**

"It's not raining!"
"The little gnome...(repeat)

"The sun is shining!"
The little gnome crept from his home, "So it is!"

Off they went to visit Short-short-long.

(repeat: Little dwarfs so short and strong...)

They came to his door.
"Now we have to find the right knock. It has to be the right one."

Do rhythms in different ways: hands clap; fingers clap; clap, clap under the leg; ears, ears mouth; head, head, knees, etc., but always the short, short, long rhythm.

At last the door opened, and there in front of them was a little gnome with a long beard and a bow tie. **B b** *The bow tie was blue with pink spots* (any colors and every time different) *and was this wide* (from sternum along collarbone) *and he loved it so much that he kept stroking it,* (short short rhythm) *and stroking his beard* (long). *Bow-tie, bow-tie, beard* (repeat), *bow, bow, beard.* (repeat rhythm)

In this way the children can do this rhythm beautifully and easily.

"Let's go to the beach and visit our friend the Lobster."

They got to the beach and went up and down the sand dunes
"Hea-vy, hea-vy, up we go!
Hea-vy, hea-vy, Oh, so slow!
Wheee! Down the other side we go."

Repeat above—heavy steps, then light,

Then they came to the rocks and the puddles. "Mustn't get wet, so copy me, careful now. Rock, rock, over a puddle." (repeat with short short long steps)

"He must be in this puddle here."

"Libster, lobster, labster lee, **i o e i**
  Living in the deep, blue sea, **i from high to low**
Libster, lobster, labster, loo, **i o e u**
Gone for tea, be back at two!" **G t b u**
(repeat using small sounds and with legs and with feet, etc.)

"Let's play some games!
We hide behind a bush. Where are you? Here we are!" **B over head, u small, A with arms and legs wide** (repeat in many ways)

"Go riding on ponies on the beach!"

Gallop to music; when the music stops, the ponies must not move. Or if there is no music and the teacher sings, "Gallop and gallop and (3x) along." When she claps, the ponies stop. One can even do it as a game where the last one who moves has to sit down.

Then the gnomes were so tired that they lay down under a tree and went to sleep.

THE TURNIP ✈
Adapted for Eurythmy

Once upon a time there was a little old man, the grandfather, **l d**
a little old lady, the grandmother, **l d**
a little girl, the grandchild, **l**
a black and white cat, **c t shoulders**
and a little mouse, **l m pointer fingers**
and they all lived together in a little house. **L small ou**

The grandfather chopped wood:
The axe swings, the steel rings ,
With a thud from below,
A sharp edge cuts a wedge,

The axe swings, the steel rings
With a bang and a clang
And a leap it bites deep.

Repeat verse; words are unimportant. Stamp and clap from side to side on long beats only.

The grandmother baked cakes:
Put in the flour, and milk, etc. **L** (children also suggest)

Mix it together **mmm**
Put it in the oven and wait. **O e**
Mmm, *smells nice.* (sniff)

The little girl, the grandchild, was:
Sweeping and cleaning and dusting all day, **W S**
Cleaning the dust and the cobwebs away. **S**
The little cat sat on the mat and purred, prrrrr (repeat). **rrrrr**
And the little mouse sniffed for cheese. "Squeee (3x) cheese (3x)." **i** (use pointer finger, then repeat with toes)

One day, the little old man the grandfather said: "I am going to plant a seed." **G A s**
"What kind of a seed?" **?**
"A turnip seed!" and they all said, **T**
"We hope it will grow!" **G O**

So up the hill went the little old man, the grandfather:
"Here I'm going up the hill...to plant my turnip seed." (London Bridge tune)
"This is the way I hack the ground, (3x) **k***...to plant my turnip seed."* (Mulberry Bush tune) **s**
"Hack (3x), hack my little hoe, Weeds (3x) all the weeds must go!" **k i G**

"This is the way I rake the ground," etc. **r**
"Rick, rack, rake, All the lumps must break, **r**
Here we go, to-and-fro, rick, rack, rake."

Now we plant the seed and say our magic verse: **s**
"Father sun, shine on our seed and make it grow, **A O**
Sister rain, rain on our seed and make it grow, **R O**
Brother Wind, blow on our seed and make it grow." **W O**

And it did grow! It grew, and it grew, and it grew and it grew, until it became suuuuch a big turnip! **U B**
One day the little old man, the grandfather, said, "Wife, put the pot on the stove, I am going to pull up the turnip!" **O T**
He went up the hill. "Now I'm going (up the hill) (3x) etc. (Mulberry Bush or music)
The little old man, the grandfather, grabbed hold of the turnip leaves **B**, *and he pulled* **oo** *(5x) and he couldn't pull up the turnip.* **Neg.**

"Little old lady, the grandmother," he called. "Come and help me pull up the turnip!" **M inwards**

Out of the house came the little old lady, the grandmother (slower walk). The little old lady, the grandmother, grabbed hold of the little old man, the grandfather **B**; *the little old man, the grandfather, grabbed hold of the turnip leaves (and they pulled) (5x) but they couldn't pull up the turnip!*

"Little girl the grandchild," she called...skipped. The little girl, the grandchild, grabbed...turnip! "Black and white cat...help to pull up the turnip!"

Out of the house came the black and white cat with her tail up in the air as all cats do when they are pleased...prrrrr prrrrrr (large **R** arms and legs with walking). *The black and white cat grabbed...turnip!*

"Mousie, mousie **m (hands)**, *come* **M** *and help to pull up the turnip!" Out of the house scampered the little mouse (on toes and fingers as whiskers).*

In time, the following can be said very fast. but with clear diction.

And so: the mouse grabbed hold of the little black and white cat; the black and white cat grabbed hold of the little girl, the grandchild, the little girl, the grandchild grabbed hold of the little old lady, the grandmother, the little old lady, the grandmother, grabbed hold of the little old man, the grandfather, (each time a new **B**) *and all together they pulled and they pulled (5x)* **U** *and* **U-P** *came the turnip.*

The little black and white cat fell on top of the little mouse, the little girl, the grandchild, fell on top of the black and white cat. The little old lady, the grandmother, fell on top of the little girl, the grandchild. The little old man, the grandfather, fell on top of the little old lady, the grandmother, and on TOP of them all fell the turnip! **T** (each time a **downward going F**, but be careful to keep upright or some children may fall down on the floor) *And they laughed "Ha, ha!"* (repeat—use **H shoulders down into A**)

They put the turnip into a big cart, and they rolled the cart home, and it was h e a v y! **R R heavy** *When they got home, they cut up the turnip,* **kkk small** *put it into a big pot, made a fire under it* **f f f from floor up** *and it bubbled, and bubbled (repeat).* **small b's with hands** (each child cups his hands and the teacher ladles soup into them) *"And there was enough soup for everybody. For you, and for you, and for you, and for me!"*

THERE WAS AN OLD LADY

Fly, fly, buzzing high, **F**
Fly, fly, through the sky.
Flittering, flying, flittering by,
Flittering, flying, up in the sky.

Sing:
There was an old lady, who swallowed a fly, **D W to mouth**
I don't know why, she swallowed the fly, **neg.**
Perhaps she'll die. **D down**

"I'm a spindly, spindly spider. **P**
I spin and spin my web,
And when I finish spinning,
I spider (or spindle) home to bed."

There was an old lady, who swallowed a spider,
It wriggled and wriggled and jiggled inside her, **r shoulders vigorously**
She swallowed the spider to catch the fly, **P f**
I don't know why she swallowed the fly,
Perhaps she'll die.

Little bird fly though the air, **L around the circle**
Fly here, fly there, fly everywhere.
Fly over mountains, fly over sea,
Fly over you and fly over me. (tweetie-wee, tweetie-wee, tweetie-wee) **i fingers**

There was an old lady, she swallowed a bird,
How absurd, to swallow a bird,
She swallowed the bird, to catch the spider, (repeat movements)
She swallowed the spider to catch the fly,
I don't know why she swallowed the fly,
Perhaps she'll die.

A big black cat sat on the mat, prrrrr prrrrr, (can cross legs and arms for each **e**) **r**
The cat on the mat was black and fat, prrrrr prrrrr,
He licked the milk and he licked the cream, **L with tongue**
And then lay down and began to dream, prrr prrr prrr prrrr. **rrr**

There was an old lady, who swallowed a cat, **k t shoulders**
Fancy that, she swallowed a cat,
She swallowed the cat to catch the bird,
She swallowed the bird to catch the spider,

She swallowed the spider, to catch the fly,
I don't know why she swallowed the fly,
Perhaps she'll die.

There was a big, big, dog."Wooof!" **B D WF**
Who lay down near a log. "Wooof!" **Low L WF**
He ate his big, big bone. "Wooof!" **B WF**
Then crept into his home. "Wooof!" **O WF**

There was an old lady, who swallowed a dog, **D**
What a hog, to swallow a dog,
She swallowed the dog to catch the cat...die.

On the mountain lived a goat. "Baaa!" **Gt e**
With two horns here, and a shaggy coat. "Baaa!" **H at head sh**
He jumped and sprang and trotted along. **P trot**
His steps were light, but soon he was gone! Because?

There was an old lady who swallowed the goat,
She opened her throat and swallowed the goat, **O**
She swallowed the goat to catch the dog...die.
Mrs. Cow lived on a farm. "Moooo!" **M U out**
She was full of love and did no harm. "Moooo!" **L**
She made her milk so warm and creamy, bend over and do **Mm** *as if from udder*
And when she was milked, she became so dreamy.

There was an old lady who swallowed a cow,
I don't know how she swallowed a cow,
She swallowed the cow to catch the goat...die.

Horsie, horsie, don't you stop, (gallop)
Just let your hooves go clippety-clop,
Your tail goes swish, and the wheels go round,
Giddy-up, we're homeward bound. "Nee-ee-ee!" (neigh)

There was an old lady who swallowed a horse,
She's dead, of course.
And out came the horse, "Nee-ee-ee!", the goat, "Baaaa!", the dog, "Wooof!", the cat, "Prrr,
prrr!", the bird, "Tweetie-wee!", the spider and the fly!
That's the end of the story, so we say, "Good bye."

RAINY WEATHER ↝

Created by a eurythmy student

Morning has come,
Night is away,
Rise with the sun,
And welcome the day.

It was early in the morning when Father Sun sent his rays to greet Mother Earth.
Two children came out of their house to play in the garden.

Ring a ring o'rosies,
A pocket full of posies,
A tishoo, A tishoo,
We all fall down!

A tishoo over the water,
A tishoo over the sea,
A tishoo over the chimney-pot
And up jump we! clap, clap on the floor, jump up

While they were playing, they heard Brother Wind blowing:
"I am the wind, **All W**
I breeze and blow,
I'm in the tree,
Listen to me,
Now I'm calling Sister Rain,
To come greet Mother Earth again."

The two children looked at each other and said,
"Quickly, quickly homeward skip,
Otherwise we'll drip, drip, drip!
Lou, lou, skip-to-my-lou, (3x)
Skip-to-my-lou my darling." (repeat twice in circle, changing direction half way)

When they arrived home they ran straight to the window because they wanted to see how
Sister Rain would come that day. While they were waiting they heard (stamp feet on the
floor several times) *thunder! Then they saw lightning (ZZZZZ), then down came the rain-*
drops.

Pitter-patter, (2x) listen to the rain,
Pitter-patter, (2x) there it goes again. (kneel and drum finger-tips quietly on the floor)
Rain, (4x) on the rooftops. (2x) POURING! (kneel and smack palms of hands on the
floor in rhythm to words; repeat with sitting and soles of the feet smack the floor,
then also with fingertips)

Then the rain stopped, so they went into the kitchen to help their mother. They washed the
dishes, then dried them and put them in the cupboard. (can sing: "This is the way we
wash the dishes...to *Mulberry Bush*)

They went outside again, but now they had to put their feet down very carefully because
the earthworms were all wriggling happily in the wet earth, and they didn't want to hurt
them.

As they were walking, they saw a spider climbing up the wall of their house.
"Incy, wincy spider, climbing up the spout, finger movements to match
Down came the rain and washed the spider out,
Out came the sun and dried up all the rain,
Incy, wincy spider climbed up the spout again."

"Children, it's getting cold outside!" It was Mommy calling. Home they skipped.

"This is the way we skip home to bed...but first we want our food!"
What a nice supper Mommy had cooked, nice hot soup and brown bread and butter!
(fold hands)

"Earth who gave to us this food,
Sun who made it ripe and good,
Never, dearest earth and sun,
Will we forget what you have done, and thank you, Brother Wind for calling Sister Rain,
for without her NOTHING grows! Amen!"

Beginning Verses

The Earth is Firm Beneath My Feet

The Earth is firm beneath my feet,
The sun shines bright above,
And here I stand, straight and strong,
All things to know and love.

We Thank Thee

R.W. Emerson

Choose whichever verse is preferred.

For flowers that bloom about our feet,
For tender grass so fresh, and sweet,
For song of bird, and hum of bee,
For all things that we hear and see,
Father in heaven, we thank Thee.

For blue of stream and blue of sky,
For pleasant shade of branches high,
For fragrant air and cooling breeze,
For beauty of the blooming trees
Father in heaven, we thank Thee.

For this new morning with its light,
For rest and shelter of this night,
For health and food, for love and friends,
For everything Thy goodness sends,
Father in heaven, we thank Thee.

We Love One Another

We love one another. **I O A**

In a circle repeat several times, but each time taking one step to center until the final
O can be done with arms around each other on either side, thereby forming one big
O together.

I Am Here

I am here, Here we are, **I A O**
We love each other so.
(same instruction as above)

Thank You for the World So Sweet

Thank you for the world so sweet,
Thank you for the food we eat,
Thank you for the birds that sing,
Thank you, God, for everything.

The Lovely Sun is Shining

The lovely sun is shining,
Up in the sky so blue,
Good morning, happy morning,
Good morning sun to you.

In All I Say

In all I say, in all I do,
May strength and kindness,
Shine right through.

Good Morning, Dear Earth

Good morning, dear Earth,
Good morning, dear sun,
Good morning, dear stones,
And flowers, everyone,
Good morning, dear beasties,
And birds on the tree
Good morning to you,
And good morning to me.

The heavens above

The heavens above, the earth below,
The angels flying to and fro,
And on the earth so firm I stand,
I stretch out my hands to greet my friends,
Good morning, (3x) everyone.

The Sun is Everybody's Friend

The sun is everybody's friend,
He warms the earth from end to end,
And he warms us every day,
Chasing all the cold away.

Guarded from Harm

Guarded from harm,   **A**
Cared for by Angels,   **E**
Here stand we,   **I**
Loving and strong   **O**
Truthful and good.   **U**

All Things Bright and Beautiful

All things bright and beautiful,
All creatures great and small
All things wise and wonderful,
The Lord God made them all.

Wheresoever I May Be

Wheresoever I may be,
God the Father is with me.
Each little flower that opens
Each little bird that sings
He made their glowing colors
He made their tiny wings.

IIn Heaven Shines a Golden Star

In heaven shines a golden star
An angel brought me from afar
From heaven high unto the earth
And brought me to my house of birth
Welcome, welcome, oh golden day
With sunshine bright and flowers gay
Where painted birds do sing their song
And make me good and kind and strong.

I See the Sun

I see the sun, and the sun sees me
I see the moon, and the moon sees me
I see my star, and my star sees me
I see you, and you see me.
(can be done as contraction and expansion, the circle going out and in)

Good Morning, Dear Earth

Good morning, dear earth,
Good morning, dear sun
Good morning, dear wide world.

The Blue Sky Above Me

The blue sky above me,
The firm earth below me,
And here stand I.

Drawing To A Close

I Can Turn Myself

I can turn myself and turn myself
And curl up when I will.
I reach on tip-toe very high
And then I stand quite still.

Jack Hall

Jack Hall, he is so small, a mouse could eat him hat and all.
Jack Dall, he is so tall, o'er mountain tops his feet do fall.
Jack Pratt, he is so fat, from side to side as fat as that.
Jack Fin, thin as a pin, if there's a crack he'd surely drop in.

Every Night an Angel Stands

Every night an angel stands, at the head of every child.
Silent, with protecting hands, it is as if he smiled,
Safely you may rest all night, in the shelter of his wings.
While in heaven's golden light, all the angels sing.

I Wiggle My Fingers

I wiggle my fingers, I wiggle my toes,
I wiggle my shoulders, I wiggle my nose,
No more wiggles are left in me
So I'll be still as still can be.

Safe I Am

Safe I am, safe I'll be
Protected by my angel.

Two Little Hands Go Clap

Two little hands go clap, clap, clap.
Two little feet go tap, tap, tap.
Two little hands go thump, thump, thump.
Two little feet go jump, jump, jump.
Two little hands go round and round.
Two little feet stand still on the ground.

WHEN THE CHILDREN GO TO SLEEP

When the children go to sleep
Stars in heaven softly peep
And the winged angels white
Watch o'er us with shining light.
(or: Watch o'er us throughout the night.)

BIRDS IN THE AIR

Birds in the air,
Stones on the land
Fishes in the water,
I am in God's Hand

I CAN GO ON TIP-TIP-TOE

I can go on tip-tip-toe,
Like the fairies I can go. (tip-toe)
I can go so you would say an elephant is on its way (stamp to each syllable).
I can rrrunnn and I can hop,
And I can spin just like a top,
I put my arms out far and wide,
And I can sway from side to side, (See-Saw, Marjorie Daw)
I can make myself so tall (tip-toe, arms high)
I can make myself so small.
I can kneel without a sound,
And sit cross-legged on the ground.
(or: And I can stand as quiet as a mouse.)

Weather Verses

Light Little, Bright Little Snowflakes
Fried Geuter

Light little, bright little, white little snowflakes,
Fair little, rare little, dear little snowflakes.
Falling so faerily, floating so airily,
Light little, bright little, white little snowflakes, ah!

With a Drip, Drip, Drip

With a drip, drip, drip and a drop, drop, drop.
See the rain on the pane, will it stop, stop, stop.
With a wink, wink, wink, and a blink, blink, blink.
Will the sun shine again do you think, think, think.

Rain, Rain, Go Away

Rain, rain, go away
Come again another day
The rain is gone, the sun is out,
Come and play and dance about.

Rain on the Green Grass

Rain on the green grass,
Rain on the tree,
Rain on the rooftops,
BUT NOT ON ME! (bend down and cover head with **B**)

The Little Gnome Creeps from his Home

The little gnome creeps from his home.
"M'thinks I hear some raindrops near,
Drip, drop, drip, drop, drizzle on the tree-top
Rain (4x) I go back in my home again."

Ha, Ha, Laughs the Wind

Ha, ha, laughs the wind,
I am up in the trees.
I am here, I am there,
In the storm, in the breeze.

There's a Great Big Storm Around

Wessel v. d. Berg

There's a great big storm around
Breaking branches to the ground,
Waving windy leaves about
Making sure no one's about.
Inside, I am in my bed
With a blanket o'er my head.
Outside, there is still a storm,
Inside, I am nice and warm.

Pitter Patter

The children love this verse, which can be used for any rainy day.

(all kneel and drum fingertips on the floor/carpet)
"Pitter patter, pitter patter, listen to the rain (pause and listen to the soft rain—fingertips)
Pitter patter, patter patter, on the windowpane.
Pitter patter, pitter patter, there it goes again."
(same kneeling position and slap hands onto floor/carpet in time to the rhythm)
"Rain, (4x) on the rooftops, rain (4x) on the rooftops,
Pouring..." (slap hands quickly)

Sit with knees bent and use toes on floor. Repeat "Pitter patter" as above using toes, then soles of feet. Now combine fingertips and toes, then palms and soles, and at the end say. "Sto-o-orming." instead of "Pouring."

The above is very good for coordination and strong limb-movements.

DWARF VERSES

LITTLE DWARFS SO SHORT AND STRONG

Little dwarfs so short and strong,
Heavy footed march along
Every head is straight and proud,
Every step is firm and loud.
Pick and hammer each must hold
Deep in earth to mine the gold.
Ready over each one's back
Hangs an empty little sack.
When the hard day's work is done,
Home again they march as one.
Each one has a heavy load
As they tramp along the road.

WE WILL WORK

We will work with a will,
With our strength, with our skill.
With a clash and a clang,
On the rocks we will bang.
For Christmas, one can add:
We will mold with our love
For the child up above
Crown so bright, made of light
Full of joy and delight.
Air: We breathe, we blow, through air we go
We dream, we stream, through air agleam.
Water: Cool in the pool, wavey and blue,
Water so soft, rain from aloft.
Fire: We flicker and flare, we flame in the air
Our sparks they fly, to the sky so high.

HE FILLS HIS SACK

He fills his sack, the little gnome,
With gold and silver, precious stone.
He ties his sack so tight and strong
Then takes it to the wood along.

Trample Trip

Trample trip, trample trot.
Clatter click—round the clock.
Hammer, pick—quick (3x)
Hit the rock—knock (3x)
Rolling rocks groan and grumble
Dwarfs are working, hear them rumble
How they laugh so merrily
Hah, hah, hah and hee, hee, hee,
Hop and dance in a row
Hee, hee, hee, off they go.

Verses for a Dragon Story

Out of the Surging Sea

Out of the surging sea
Slinky and slimy
Creeping and crawling
Raging and roaring
The dragon is here!
See how it opens its yawning jaws
See how it scrapes its scaly claws.

Children can hold onto the one in front and follow the teacher as a snake while the teacher does the movements.

Up on the Broom

Up on the broom the witches stream
Crooked and black in the crimson gleam
One foot high and one foot low
Bearded, cloaked and cowled they go.

The children love being witches with dramatic movements.

VERSES TO MAKE THE CHILDREN HELPERS OF ST. MICHAEL

I Am Strong, I Am Brave

I am strong, I am brave,
I am valiant and bold,
For the sun fills my heart
With its life-giving gold.
I am helpful and truthful, and loving and free
For the sun's golden rays do shine brightly in me.
I will open my heart to the sun's warming might
I will fill all the world with my heart's living light.

Brave and True

Brave and true will I be,
Each good deed sets me free.
Each kind thought makes me strong.
I will fight for the right,
I will conquer the wrong.

Go! Go! Go!

Go! Go! Go! Dragon you must go!
Or, we will prick you,
We will stick you,
We will race you, we will chase you!
Go! Go! Go! Dragon you must go!

Horses

Horse Training School

The children ask for this over and over and cannot get enough of it. This can be used for many stories or even on its own with another long action verse. The children sit against a wall where they can watch and there must be a fair amount of space.

Put out 8 small chairs or copper rods in the following way:

```
 1   1    XX    1   1

          XX           X = children

 1   1    XX    1   1
```

It is best to start with two children who are competent. The others watch and learn through imitation. They hold hands and walk up the aisle from the back. At the front they release hands, one goes to the right and the other to the left. Keeping level with their partners they go around the chairs, straight line to the back, around the back chairs and to the back center aisle where they hold hands again.

Then only two more children are chosen and follow the front ones up the aisle, etc. It is important every time children are added to ask them to point to the ones they are going to follow. In this way, they will not get lost. The teacher stands at the top of the aisle and marks time and sings, or there is marching music. From there it is easier to divide off the children if there is any confusion.

Very slowly add two more at a time. If there is an odd number, the odd one can be the "leader."

When they can all manage, one can enter more into the fantasy of horse-training or circus training–putting imaginary feathers in their manes, i.e. knees up, trotting, etc.

At the end, the teacher can tell the horses to stand in a circle in front of their stable doors while she turns her back and counts to three slowly. Then she joins them, and all say **Brrrrrrrrr** (with tongue and lips as a horse) and **R** with hoof, and, "Neeeee." Then the teacher gives each one a lump of sugar.

Musical Horses

A game at the end of a lesson

The children are allowed to gallop freely and when the music stops they have to stop and the last one has to sit down. To avoid "competition," the ones who sit have to help observe, so they still feel involved. It also helps to have three "last" horses and not a "winner."

Horsie, Horsie

Horsie, horsie, don't you stop,
Just let your hoofs go clippety-clop.
Your tail goes swish, and the wheels go round,
Giddy-up, we're homeward bound.

Galloping

A horse flies on the silver track
Hoofs high in the air, and not looking back.
You, flying there so free and proud,
Among the stars, next to a cloud.
Seek you a rider, let it be me.
(To Bethlehem fly, the child to see)
To fly over mountain, fly over sea.
Carry me, horse, so free and proud,
Among the stars, next to a cloud.

GENERAL VERSES

THE WEDDING

The blackbirds had a wedding fine
And all the birds were asked to dine.
Tira la la la, Tira le le le,
Tira li li lo lo loo.
The robin in his waistcoat red
He'd baked a wedding cake of bread,
(Repeat Tira la...)
The woodpecker came with a tat,tat,tat,
All dressed up in his best red hat,
(Repeat Tira la...)
The lark came with his loveliest song
And whistled it the whole day long
(Repeat Tira la...)
The duck came in his eiderdown,
It's very cold they say in town.
(Repeat Tira la...)
Coo, coo, coo, coo, said the turtle-dove
I bring you lots and lots of love.
(Repeat Tira la...)

SHOPPING

There was a young lady went into a shop
Hippety, hoppity, hippety, hop.
She filled up her basket with eggs to the top,
Tippety, toppety, tippety top.
When she walked out she let it all drop,
Drippety, droppity, drippety, drop.
The bread and the butter fell down with a flop,
Flippety, floppity, flippety, flop.
And one of the bottles went off with a pop,
Pippety, poppety, pippety, pop.
The cat jumped down from the tabletop,
Lippety, loppety, lippety lop.
The shopkeeper cleaned it all up with a mop.
Mippety, moppity, mippety, mop.
And that's the end of the story,
and now we must stop.

27
OVER IN THE MEADOW

Over in the meadow in the sand and the sun
Lived a big mother frog and her little froggy one,
"Hop," said the mother. "I hop," said the one,
So they hopped and they hopped in the sand and the sun.

Over in the meadow where the stream flows so blue
Lived a big mother fish and her little fishies two,
"Swim," said the mother. "We swim," said the two,
So they swam and they swam where the stream flows so blue.

Over in the meadow in the big oak tree,
Lived a big mother bird and her little birdies three.
"Fly," said the mother. "We fly." said the three,
So they flew and they flew in the big oak tree.

Over in the meadow in the reeds by the shore,
Lived a big mother rat and her little ratties four,
"Dive," said the mother. "We dive,"said the four,
So they dived and they dived in the reeds by the shore.

Over in the meadow in the sunny beehive
Lived a big queen bee and her little bees five.
"Bzzz," said the queen. "We bzzz," said the five,
So they bzzzd and they bzzzd round the sunny beehive.

UNDER THE STONE

Under the stone where the earth was firm,
I found a wriggly, wriggly worm.
"Good morning," I said, "How are you today?"
But the wriggly worm, he just wriggled away,
He wriggled away. (2x)
The wriggly worm, he just wriggled away.
Nearby the stone where the earth is wider,
I saw a long-legged spindly spider.
"Good morning," I said, "How are you today?"
But the long-legged spider, he spun away,
He spun away, (2x)
The long-legged spider, he spun away.

Nearby the church near the tall, tall steeple
I saw a big black grabbly beetle.
"Good morning," I said, "How are you today?"
But the grabbly beetle, he just grabbled away,
He grabbled away, (2x)
The grabbly beetle, he just grabbled away.
There near the beehive, what did I see?
A busy buzzing, buzzing bee.
"Good morning," I said, "How are you today?"
But the buzzing bee he just bzzzd away,
He bzzzd away, (2x)
The buzzing bee, he just bzzzd away.
Out in the garden, know what I heard?
A lovely, singing, soaring bird.
"Good morning," I said, "How are you today?"
And the singing bird he just flew away,
He flew away (2x)
The singing bird, he just flew away.

1,2,3, MUMMY CAUGHT A FLEA

1,2,3, Mummy caught a flea
Daddy caught a bigger one,
And put it in his tea.
When he put the milk in, it floated to the top
When he put the sugar in, the flea went pop!

Clap on 1,2,3 and pop.

I CAN WIND A BALL OF WOOL

I can wind a ball of wool, a ball of wool, a ball of wool,
I can wind a ball of wool, and this is the way I do it.
S-l-o-w-l-y wind the ball of wool, do it.
Quickly wind, do it.

STEPPING OVER STEPPING STONES

Stepping over stepping stones, 1 2 3
Stepping over stepping stones just like me,
Stepping over stepping stones happy as can be,
Stepping over stepping stones light and free.
One step, two step, give a little hop,
Loud step, soft step, find it hard to stop.
Long step, short step, spin just like a top,
Fat step, thin step, let your hands go plop!

ALLE MALLE MINK-MONK

Alle malle mink-monk, tink-tonk toozy
Oozy voozy aggedy, ah vah vek!

Make up a hand game, e.g. roll hands around each other, point, clap, etc.

28
BYE, LITTLE ONE, BYE

Bye, little one, bye,
Mummy is making the baby's bed,
While Daddy is working for daily bread,
Bye, little one, bye, bye,
Bye, little one, bye.

THE SUN SAYS I GLOW

The sun says, "I glow."
The wind says, "I blow."
The stream says, "I flow."
The tree says, "I grow."
And Man says, "I know."

29

There in the Woods I See a Tree

There in the woods, I see a tree,
The loveliest tree you ever did see,
And the green leaves grew around, around, around,
And the green leaves grew around.
There in the tree, I see a nest,
The loveliest nest you ever did see (repeat as above verse)
There in the nest I see four eggs, etc.
Then from the eggs there came four birds, etc.

Baking

Flour and butter do I take,
Egg and milk to make a cake
From the hive I have some honey
Nice and sticky, not so runny.
Nuts and raisins, eggs and spice
Chocolate chips to make things nice.
Not too wet and not too dry
Take this finger and we try.
Now the dough we mix and tumble
Mix it so it does not crumble.
In the oven now so hot (big sniffs)
Three big cakes, we bake the lot.

Magic Wood Spiral

This can be used in many stories and the children are always amazed at the "magic."

First start off by asking the children to note who is on either side of them, and take special note which child is on the side of your ring (or watch). Then lead them into and out of a large spiral so that all end up facing outward. Then all jump around to face the center of the circle and see how the places have changed!

We're Going Through the Magic Wood

We're going through (the Magic Wood) (2x)
We're going through the Magic Wood,
That turns us inside out!

Contraction And Expansion

To Market, to Market

To market, to market to buy a fat pig,
Home again, home again, jiggety jig.
To market, to market to buy us some bread,
Home again, home again, jump into bed.

With the first line, contract the circle into the center while stamping; then, on the second line, expand the circle with everyone on tip-toe, holding hands. Repeat, but each time buy something else and make up a rhyme to match.

Now Up So High

Now up so high, now down so low
Up in the air, downward we go,
Up in the sky, down on the grass,
See the birds fly, see the ants pass.

The Leaves Said It's Spring

The leaves said, "It's spring, and here are we, (circle expands out)
Opening and stretching on every tree."
The leaves said, "It's summer, each bird has a nest, (in)
And we make the shade in which they can rest."
The leaves said, "It's autumn and we are all gay," (out)
Scarlet and gold and russet are they.
The leaves said, "It's winter, and tired are we," (in)
So they lay down to rest underneath a tree.

Sleep, Sleep, Sleep, Little Seed

Sleep, sleep, sleep, little seed,
Sleep through the winter long.
Wake (2x) in the spring,
Wake with the bluebird's song.
Sleep (2x) little seed
Hidden from sight away.
Wake, wake, waken and grow,
Waken for summer's day.

Light in a Blossom

Jean Lynch

Start in a small circle and a small **L**. With each growing one take small step back or stand in circle and let **L**'s grow.

Light in a blossom (or raindrop)
Light in candle flame,
Light in a lantern,
Light through windowpane
Light of the silver moon,
Light of starry skies,
And the Light of all the world
That lights up people's eyes.

14

Wake Up

Wake up, wake up, the sun shines bright,
The dark is conquered by the light.

Go To Sleep Now

Go to sleep now, little darling,
Night is coming blue and deep,
Stars are bright and angels carry
Down from heaven holy sleep
Aaiya (2x) down from heaven holy sleep.

Because the R belongs so much to the squirrel, it can be exaggerated and rolled on

Colored Veils

These are suitable for Spring and Summer

There Are Big Waves and Little Waves

Have enough small veils of different rainbow colors so that each child can have one. measurements approximately: 16 square inches (40 centimeters).

When they are sitting in a circle, put one down in front of each child. Show them how to feel its softness against their cheeks. Let them hold two corners and together practice going in and out of the circle together, waving it like big and little waves, and then waving from side to side.

There are big waves (in and out of circle)
And little waves,
And green waves, and blue (side to side)
Waves you can jump over (jump with veils up)
Waves you dive through **U** (veil from low to up over head)
Waves that rise up like a big water wall (into circle as a big wave)
Waves that swell softly and don't break at all (out of circle with small waves)
Waves that can whisper (soft small waves side to side)
And waves that can roar (large side-to-side movements)
And tiny waves that run at you, running on the shore. (running on toes around the circle in little waves)

Caterpillar Wind About

Scarves can be placed in a spiral with colors graded according to the verse used. The following can be done by one child at a time:

Caterpillar wind about, round and round and in and out,
When you're fed, spin your bed,
Caterpillar die, (in center of spiral) *waken as a butterfly!*
Rise from death, and unfold,
Spread your soft wings of gold,
Upward fly to the light,
Bringing joy and delight.

Into the Cave I find My Way

Into the cave I find my way,
And with my blessed angel stay.
Then from out my cave I go
To bring God's light to all I know.

The veils can also be placed as stairs of a rainbow and the children step over the colors without touching them.

1
Here We Go on Tip-toe

Here we go on tip-toe (hopping so, etc.), *over the rainbow bridge we go*
Stepping (hopping) *softly stepping* (hopping) *slow, over the rainbow bridge we go.*
Up into the heavens far, gathering light from sun and star
Down to earth all things to greet,
Bringing light to all we greet.

MUSIC FOR NUMBERED VERSES

1. Here we go, on tip-toe.

2. Adam he had 7 sons.

3. This is the way to.......

4. Roses

5. Puffer train

Sshh 4

Sshh 4

6. Kirri (2) ki

7. Ding Dong

8. In our Springtime Garden

9. There in the woods......

10. Waken sleeping butterfly,

11. Weaving nest

12. Fly butterfly

13. Gnomes.

14. Wake up (2)

15. Big Fat Caterpillar

16. Go to sleep now

17. Shake (2) the apple tree

18. Ring Glocklein

19. Blue Boat

20. Have you seen the little ducks

21. A prince-riding

22. Pancake - fire fire....

23. Pancake - see the lovely......

24. Pancake - I jumped out of......

25. Golden goose Walk along

26. Golden goose 2 Help.....

27. Over the meadow

28. B M D

29. Autumn leaves

REFERENCES

(some of which have been adapted by E. Bryer)

Aulie, Jennifer and Margret Meyerkort (Eds.). *Spring; Summer; Autumn; Winter; Spindrift;* and *Gateways* (a series of six collections of poems, songs and stories for young children), Stourbridge, UK: Wynstones Press, 1999. Also, *Songs of Sunfield,* currently out of print.

Foster, Nancy. *Let Us Form a Ring: An Acorn Hill Anthology,* Silver Spring, MD: Acorn Hill Children's Center, 1989.

Foster, Nancy. *Dancing As We Sing: Seasonal Circle Plays & Traditional Singing Games,* Silver Spring, MD: Acorn Hill Children's Center, 1999.

Harwood, A.C. *The Way of the Child.*

Steiner, Rudolf. *Education for Special Needs* (The Curative Education Course).

Steiner, Rudolf. *Understanding Young Children, Excerpts from Lectures compiled for Kindergarten Teachers,* Waldorf Early Childhood Association, 1993.

Thienes-Schunemann, Mary. *Sing a Song of Seasons; The Singing Baby; This is the Way We Wash-a-Day; The Wonder of Lullabies* (four volumes from the "Singing With Children Series), E. Troy, WI: Naturally You Can Sing Productions, 2000-03.

Von Heydebrand, Caroline. *Childhood: A Study of the Growing Soul,* Steiner Books, 1995.